1989

Careers
in
Video

Getting Ahead
in Professional
Television

Ken Jurek

Knowledge Industry Publications, Inc.
White Plains, New York

Video Bookshelf

Careers in Video:
Getting Ahead in Professional Television

Library of Congress Cataloging-in-Publication Data

Jurek, Ken.
    Careers in video.

    (Video bookshelf)
    Bibliography: p.
    Includes index.
    1. Video recordings—Production and direction—
Vocational guidance. 2. Employees, Training of—
Audio-visual aids—Vocational guidance. I. Title.
II. Series.
PN1992.94.J87   1988   791.45'023'023   88-34521
ISBN 0-86729-169-9

Printed in the United States of America

10   9   8   7   6   5   4   3   2   1

To Muffy and the two Ilonas,

who always were there.

Contents

List of Figures vi
Acknowledgments vii
Introduction ix

1   Applications of Nonbroadcast Television   1
2   Nonbroadcast Television Today   9
3   The Nonbroadcast Television Marketplace 29
4   Looking for a Job in Video 69
5   Preparing for an Interview 91
6   Handling Interview Questions 105
7   Resumes, Qualifications Briefs and Resume Reels 131
8   Finding a New Job 155
9   Career Paths in Nonbroadcast Video 181
10 Moving Out of Nonbroadcast Video 223

Appendix A: Organizations that Actively Use Video 236
Appendix B: Salary Surveys 251
Appendix C: Professional Organizations 253
Bibliography 261
Index 263
About the Author 267

List of Figures

Figure 1.1: On location shooting of a scene from "Reliance
Electric Presents the Basics of Gearing" 3

Figure 2.1: Programming an interactive videodisc 19
Figure 2.2: Dave Phillips preparing a studio shoot for a
sales program 26

Figure 3.1: Filming a corporate news program 43
Figure 3.2: AVID Productions' control room 61
Figure 3.3: Freelance producer working with two freelance
production assistants 62

Figure 4.1: Volunteer experience led to a career in medical
video for Maria Keckan 76

Figure 7.1: Sample resume for a newcomer to the
nonbroadcast video industry 134
Figure 7.2: Sample resume for an advanced position in
nonbroadcast video 136
Figure 7.3: Qualifications brief #1: employment history ... 145
Figure 7.4: Qualifications brief #2: educational
background 146
Figure 7.5: Qualifications brief #3: miscellaneous
accomplishments 147

Figure 9.1: Cameraperson, Joan Dollard, readies her
camera to film the training segment of a
news program 185

Acknowledgments

When I started to write this book, I had no idea of the journey that lay ahead. There are a number of individuals who helped in my most dire moments of need and who assisted in teaching me what it takes to put together a book of this magnitude. Ellen Lazer, senior editor, is the person who stood with me the longest on this project, and pushed me when I needed it. Editor Laurie Nevin picked up the ball and kept me racing to the finish line.

Over the years, I have gathered information, stories and ideas from the many people mentioned, footnoted and quoted in this book. They have been both my unwavering support group and sounding board and I appreciate all of them for their assistance.

But, the one person who has pushed, prodded, coddled and cajoled me through to the end of this worthy project and who deserves as much credit for each written word as I would lay claim to is my associate, video editor and director, wife and extremely good friend, Joan Dollard-Jurek.

Introduction

It started innocently enough.

Five years ago, I volunteered to write a series of articles on employment for a couple of newsletters and video industry trade journals. I had always been in video and, because of my position with the nation's largest executive search and placement firm, I had received an exhaustive education on how one goes about finding a job. Later, the information grew and developed as I started giving speeches, workshops and seminars to nonbroadcast professionals on the art of finding a job and moving up the career ladder.

While meeting and working with the many talented people in this industry, I received one message over and over again.

That message was that while the professionals in our industry know a great deal about television and communication, they know little about marketing their skills to look for a position. And those who had positions and wanted to move up or out had little idea as to how to prepare themselves for the job search.

The people who attended my seminars were in the media or, at least, hoped soon to be. Either they were nonbroadcast video professionals who had helped populate the industry from its earliest days or they were students finishing college who wanted to join the video ranks but knew little about the nonbroadcast television industry.

Often, they came to the seminars hesitatingly and, at first, were unsure of what to expect. Looking for a job requires some aggressiveness and confidence, two traits that many of us lack. But, soon after I started explaining the industry and how to compile a contact list, they flipped open their notebooks and started to take notes. The job search concepts coupled with the nonbroadcast television information struck an exciting chord among them, and their interest grew.

Slowly, I started putting together outlines and then manuals for them to follow. It seemed that no matter how much time we had for the workshop, there were always more questions than I had time to answer. Often, after arriving home, I would receive letters asking for more information about something I had said in a speech or written in an article.

Some of the questions were basic, such as "Where can I look to find a job in nonbroadcast video?," "I have a degree and experience, but what am I qualified to do?" and "What should my resume and resume reel look like?"

Other questions were more advanced and emanated from people who had the experience and a job, but felt they could do more. Questions abounded, such as: "I've done all that I can in this job. I know I can do more . . . but where can I go, what can I do?" "I've always wanted to be a producer, but I've been stuck in this videographer position for 10 years. What should I do?" And, "I think I'd like to get out of nonbroadcast video, but where can I go?"

Employers contributed more than their fair share of questions, such as, "How can I find good, qualified people?" "What questions can I ask potential job candidates?" And, "How can I make sure that someone with the right experience is going to be a good fit for my department?"

This book approaches these questions and more from your specific point of view. It is meant as a reference guide and job search tool and is designed to answer questions for both the novice entering the field and the more experienced employee who wants to move up and/or out.

The simple fact is that nonbroadcast television is the fastest growing segment of the video industry. All indicators point to even greater growth in the coming years. Obviously, with the on-going technological changes (HDTV, desktop video, cable television, business satellite communications and the move to digital formats) and the emerging high quality of nonbroadcast programming more highly qualified personnel will be needed in the coming decades to operate this premier communications medium.

This book is designed to be a guide for all people seeking employment or career enhancement in video. It is a nuts-and-bolts guide with practical suggestions that work. It is not a book of false hope or glib phrases. It explains the strategies involved in making a career move and examines the specific challenges of the nonbroadcast video professional.

Chapters 1 and 2 outline the industry and its specific segments. They are designed to get you thinking about people and organizations and to help you inventory your background. How to find contacts, what you should do with contacts and how to conduct and market yourself in interviews will be discussed in Chapters 3 and 4.

Chapters 5, 6 and 7 are concerned with the nuts and bolts of the interviewing process: preparation, the importance of your resume and resume reel and what you should hope to accomplish during the interview. Finally, Chapters 8 and 9 detail the specific jobs and the career ladders you can take to get to where you want to go. And, should you want to move out of nonbroadcast television, Chapter 10 explains where you can go and what you are qualified to do. There are special sections on management, freelancing and starting your own cottage video industry. Freelancing and starting your own video services company are two areas that have great growth potential.

I hope the book is useful to all of you who are seeking to hone and refine your job seeking skills. Although there are other books on finding a job or writing a resume, there is only one that deals frankly with today's nonbroadcast video marketplace . . . and that is this one.

The aim of this book is to help anyone who sincerely seeks employment in nonbroadcast television. The information within is the most current and complete available. The methods described have helped countless others and are helping many more, even as you read this.

And while the potential for you in this field is limitless, there are things that I have no control over, specifically, what you do with the information and how you conduct your own search. But it is my hope that you will be successful.

1
Applications of Nonbroadcast Television

The first thing you see is a title "Remember NYSE Rule 387." It fades into a black-and-white scene of a businessman hurrying down the steps of a building. Suddenly, he stops and recognizes two people, former brokerage associates, now selling umbrellas and souvenirs from behind a stand. He remarks that they were once top stockbrokers and wonders what happened to them.

On cue the former stockbrokers start singing "Runaround Sue," an old rock-and-roll hit by Dion. The screen turns to color as the inside of a brokerage office unfolds. To the sounds of the Beach Boys' "Fun, Fun, Fun," a guitar-carrying manager, backed by a chorus of singing and dancing stockbrokers, unveils the tragic story of what happens to brokers who forget NYSE (New York Stock Exchange) Rule 387.

Produced by the Merrill Lynch corporate video department, this slick program was designed to train and inform stockbrokers about following the rules of the New York Stock Exchange, particularly Rule 387. In 1987 it was awarded the International Television Association's (ITVA) highest award for production excellence, the Golden Reel, and was publicly reviewed at the 1988 ITVA meeting in Las Vegas by *Chicago Tribune* motion picture critic Gene Siskel, who gave it his coveted "thumbs up."

* * *

At first, she speaks confidently, calmly. She discusses having children, how they always wanted children, how she got pregnant. Then she pauses. Eyes welling with tears, she starts to explain how it was in the hospital. She went in so happy . . . but then, something happened. She lost the baby. Stillborn. No, it does not help to be in a maternity ward at that time, she says. There should be somewhere else to go, apart from mothers and their newborns, where patients could receive the medical and psychological treatment they need. The credits then come up– "Stillbirth, Miscarriage, and Beyond," produced by Fairview General Hospital (1985).

* * *

The man in the trenchcoat waits. The sky is eerie, grey, ominous. Suddenly, a black limousine screeches to a halt in front of him. A briefcase is thrown toward him, he catches it and scurries off. Later, in the confines of his office as a private investigator, he examines the contents. It is a mystery. A mystery about electric motors. The title fades in—"Reliance Electric Presents the Basics of Gearing." (See Figure 1.1.)

Soon the screen turns blue and the viewer is offered a choice of training tracks: beginner, intermediate or advanced. Hundreds of newly hired engineers and salesmen learn from the tape by making this and many other choices. At various times, the training program is interrupted for an on-screen test of the viewer's progress. Throughout, this interactive video teaches necessary skills to the salesmen and engineers.

* * *

As the lights dim, the thousand-member audience quiets. You could hear a pin drop. It is obvious that something special is about to begin. Two 9-ft. by 12-ft. screens on each side of the massive stage start to illuminate; the first chords of music are heard. It is melodic, sexy and driven.

Images flash on the screens and the crowd applauds. A camera crew, joined by headsets to two directors shouting commands to various spotlight technicians, audio engineers and stage crew wait in silence for the

Figure 1.1: On Location Videotaping of "Reliance Electric Presents the Basics of Gearing."

Courtesy of Reliance Electric.

opening videotape musical number to end. The president of the company greets the audience from the podium; the crowd applauds. Then, a heavily choreographed and videotaped awards ceremony, similar to the Academy Awards, begins.

This program is produced by Management Recruiters International. Other corporations, including Federal Express, IBM, AT&T and Eastman Kodak, produce similar video extravaganzas. Designed to motivate and inform, they communicate the ideas and feelings of the organization's management. Some of these events are uplinked to satellite stations and distributed "live" to various downlink locations where the company's employees can watch.

* * *

NONBROADCAST TELEVISION DEFINED

Scenes like these are repeated every day by thousands of organizations. Although these programs are often well received by their audiences and respected in their industries, they will never be broadcast to your home. That's because they form the growing field of *nonbroadcast video.*

Nonbroadcast television is programming produced and operated for a specific entity, such as an educational institution, corporation, governmental or medical body. It sometimes goes by the names "corporate television," "private television," "organizational television" and even "nonbroadcast video." This programming often has clearly stated objectives, including training, informing, motivating, educating and communicating. Nonbroadcast television is not intended for mass distribution, but is targeted to specific audiences. Audiences that view nonbroadcast programming include an organization's employees or customers, trainees, students, engineers, doctors, nurses, stockholders and clients. Any group can comprise an audience for nonbroadcast television.

TRAINING, MOTIVATION AND INFORMATION APPLICATIONS

Nonbroadcast video has achieved acceptance as a legitimate means of delivering training, motivational, and informational communications to defined audiences. These audiences include the employees of a corporation, the students of a particular discipline, the customers of a retail establishment, a group of professionals, etc. What is evident from the studies that profile the industry is that nonbroadcast television is a growing, vital profession that impacts a greater number of industries, associations and institutions every year.[1] Chapter 2 will give you an overview of the evolution of nonbroadcast television.

---

[1] Judith Tereno Stokes, *The Business of Nonbroadcast Television* (White Plains, NY: Knowledge Industry Publications, Inc., 1988) and Judith M. and Douglas P. Brush, *Private Television Communications: The New Directions* (Cold Spring, NY: HI Press, Inc., 1986).

Like its high-technology sibling, data processing, nonbroadcast television has seen its users as well as its uses multiply. The programs created by nonbroadcast professionals are as diverse as the number and types of industries and organizations they serve. For example:

- Nonbroadcast television is used to record the underground placement of pumping equipment for sewer districts. It is also used to train employees on the proper care and operation of highly sensitive equipment.
- Nonbroadcast television is used to record and distribute details of an important stockholders' meeting to members located far from the company's headquarters. It is used to promote the value of the company's stock by compiling a "video annual report" for employees and stockholders that has more impact than the traditional written report.
- At the same time, nonbroadcast television trains the corporation's sales staff on new procedures and techniques. The corporation's entire sales and service force can view firsthand, via satellite, a new product or service. Then they can call in "live" questions and concerns to senior management from several different locations throughout the country.
- Meanwhile, nonbroadcast video is training the company's accountants on the use of the latest software spreadsheet program. Managers and their staffs are also watching off-the-shelf management, leadership or customer relations programs to improve their overall performance.
- All company personnel can learn more about the corporation by watching news and information programming provided via quarterly, monthly or weekly corporate news shows.
- A company involved in retail sales can show its products in use to prospective customers *before* they make their purchases. At the same time, nonbroadcast television will be used to explain the operation of the new cash register and inventory systems to the company's clerks. At other times, it explains how to maintain a safe environment while on the job.

- Nonbroadcast television is used in the medical field. It records the work of a physical therapist with a patient and is used to gauge both the patient's progress and the therapist's techniques. It shows how nursing homes, hospitals, and other extended-care facilities can deal with the prevention of theft or loss of residents' belongings.
- Nonbroadcast television shows the latest surgical techniques to physicians scattered throughout the world. It records a team of physicians performing a delicate multi-hour operation. Another team of physicians will be able to use the record in follow-up cases. Patients waiting for surgery are informed and reassured in their rooms by watching the hospital's local in-patient televison cable services. Patients can zero in on specific health programs, created specifically for their use.
- Nonbroadcast video can explain the new benefits program to the 35,000 employees of a public utility. It can also teach those same employees how to quickly diagnose and treat burns and other medical emergencies that may occur while on the job.
- Nonbroadcast television allows a physics student to examine the lab Alexander Graham Bell worked in to devise the telephone, so he/she can understand the thought processes involved in such a discovery. It can help that same student cram for a biology exam. It might enhance another student's forensic techniques when he/she sees recorded documentation of his/her debate performance.
- Visitors at a museum gain better understanding of exhibits by a graphic reenactment of an historic event or depiction of an artist's life. Visitors to a maritime park marvel at nonbroadcast videos showing white whales birthing in their environment. Visitors to a NASA research facility may watch as a man named Armstrong steps, for the first time, on the moon.

EXPAND YOUR OPTIONS

When looking for a job in the nonbroadcast industry, it is easy to make the mistake of narrowing the field of opportunity.

It is important that you expand it and explore all the different areas that might offer opportunities. Executive search and job placement agencies have found that people do not change jobs only for more money, but also for opportunity. To find these opportunities, it is up to you to uncover and investigate all possibilities. Chapter 3 will provide you with an overview of the many segments of the nonbroadcast television marketplace.

ENTRY-LEVEL POSITIONS

There is an unwritten rule in our industry concerning most first-time job seekers. It is "you gotta pay your dues." Therefore, you must succeed in an entry-level position before you can hope to move up the career ladder.

Use this book as a reference guide to trigger your imagination. Write down things that strike you as being part of your nature and act on them. You need to be somewhat aggressive and learn to sell yourself. If you have no experience, you have to make up for this deficiency by being willing to work anywhere, do anything, for very little or no remuneration.

This means you may have to volunteer your services, show up, offer to help out—anything to get started. As you read this chapter on the marketplace, jot down the names of any person, acquaintance, company, or institution that comes to mind. Follow up with a call, a written query or a visit. And be sure to thank them by sending a follow-up letter. The more contacts you have, the more likely your chances of finding a position will be.

Chapter 4 will provide details on how to find that important first job in nonbroadcast video. Chapter 5 will help you prepare for an interview, and Chapter 6 will show you how to deal with interview questions. Chapter 7 will discuss the importance of resumes and demonstration reels.

ADVANCED CAREER OPTIONS

After you have had some experience in nonbroadcast television, Chapter 8 will explain how to find your next position when a job change is appropriate. Career paths within our industry are discussed in Chapter 9 and, in Chapter 10, options available for making the transition from nonbroadcast to broadcast video are explained. Chapter 10 also explains how to read the "writing on the wall" that warns of changes that may affect you.

Chapter 11 discusses the marketplace and should be of particular help to those with advanced careers as you should already have a handle on specific names and acquaintances in the field. No matter how long you have been in nonbroadcast television, you have met a number of people who either have a job that is of interest to you or know of someone who does. Chapter 11 is designed to help you put together a list of people and places to contact, inquire about, and eventually talk with about what you have to offer them, while investigating their opportunities for you.

This book will show you how to achieve your goals in nonbroadcast television. Each chapter builds logically on the preceding one to show you what the next step should be. Most important, try everything and remember: YOU ARE IN NO POSITION TO TURN DOWN ANYTHING THAT MIGHT GIVE YOU NON-BROADCAST TELEVISION EXPERIENCE!!!

2
Nonbroadcast Television Today

THE EVOLUTION OF NONBROADCAST TELEVISION

Television broadcasting began to evolve in the laboratory in the 1930s. Led by such economic giants as General Electric, AT&T and RCA, television stations and then television networks began broadcasting to the general public, or, at least, to anyone who could afford to purchase the bulky, expensive television receiver.

After World War II, television stations proliferated at a dizzying rate. But, except for the occasional use of the video-to-film type of recorder known as the kinescope, television in the 1950s was live.

EARLY VIDEOTAPING

In 1956, Ampex introduced the first videotape recorder (VTR). It captured live televised events and recorded the images on 2-inch magnetic tape. The VTRs, known as quadruplex recorders because of their use of four video recording heads, were costly and cumbersome. They were huge, noisy creatures that could not be moved from their climate-controlled environs. In those days, remote programs produced in the "field" were limited by how far the studio camera cables could be stretched into the street.

9

PORTABLE VTRs

Inexpensive black-and-white VTRs and cameras began to be produced in the early 1960s. Produced by Ampex and IVC (International Video Corporation), these units could not equal the picture quality of the quads, but they weighed less. Still, one of these VTRs, the Ampex 7800, was so heavy that it became portable only when lifted by two men. The machines cost less because they used 1-inch helical (two-headed, scanned) videotape.

The 1-Inch VTRs

While only commercial television stations and a few large educational television stations could afford 2-inch VTRs, many could afford the lesser quality 1-inch equipment. Corporations and governmental units started to purchase these lower-cost units for two other reasons. First, they could record and document events. Special announcements made by a corporation president or other VIP could be recorded and played back at various company sites to the entire employee population.

Second, trainers saw the inexpensive VTRs as a way to make more of an impact. Money and time could be saved because non-broadcast programs trained employees more effectively, more thoroughly, more consistently and at more than one location at a time. The use of visuals increased trainees' understanding. When color is used with visuals, studies have shown that trainee comprehension increases by 70% and the learning process is accelerated by 78%.[1]

---

[1] See, for example, Roland E. Green, "Communicating with Color," *Audio Visual Communications* (November 1978), pp. 14–47.

The ½-Inch VTRs

On the heels of the 1-inch developments came a series of ½-inch VTRs produced by Hitachi, Sony and Panasonic. While these early VTRs were an improvement in portability over their predecessors, they suffered from a total lack of compatibility.

Incompatibility occurred when a tape recorded on a Panasonic could not be played on a Sony or Hitachi. As nonbroadcast organizations bought equipment from different manufacturers, the compatibility problem started to slow the growth of the nonbroadcast marketplace. While vendors could argue the merits of their VTRs and other equipment, it soon became apparent that many potential nonbroadcast purchasers would not commit to the medium until the compatibility problems were resolved.

Standardized Helical Formats

In 1970, standardization of nonbroadcast helical formats was formalized. The Electronics Industries Association of Japan (EIAJ) standard of 1970, known as EIAJ Type 1, set the stage for an explosion of low-cost video equipment tailored specifically to the nonbroadcast market. Now, organizations could make programs for specific audiences with the knowledge that the tapes could be played anywhere. At the same time, the demand for qualified personnel to produce these programs increased.

THE INFLUENCE OF VIDEOCASSETTES ON NONBROADCAST EQUIPMENT

Exploiting the nonbroadcast market even further, the concept of a fully contained tape unit that could be easily inserted into a video recorder for instant use evolved into reality in the form of the "videocassette." The first videocassette recorders (VCRs) entered the market in the late 1960s.

The ¾-Inch U-Matic Format

The ¾-inch format was initially designed by Japanese companies (Matsushita, Sony and JVC) as a "dummy proof" distribution format; videocassettes replaced the often unruly open tape reels. But nonbroadcast production personnel soon were so enamored with the ease of the ¾-inch recorder that they demanded its expansion into a production format.

Production Equipment

Equipment manufacturers, such as Sony, Panasonic and JVC, were only too happy to oblige in the creation of several generations of production equipment: cameras, video switchers, remote edit controllers, character generators, portable tripods, lights, audio mixing boards and microphones. The industry that portable video created helped solidify ¾-inch U-Matic as the production workhorse of the industry.[2] The ¾-inch U-Matic format, particularly with the enhanced quality the new SP models now offer, seems secure in nonbroadcast production, at least for the foreseeable future.

While manufacturers have attempted to make the ½-inch formats more advantageous to production use, these formats– e.g., 8mm, Betacam and M formats– are relatively new and have yet to make much impact on the nonbroadcast video market.[3]

Portable Equipment

Portable equipment helped break nonbroadcast video out of the studio and into the outside world. No longer were large and

---

[2] Judith M. and Douglas P. Brush, *Private Television Communications: The New Directions* (Cold Spring, NY: HI Press, 1986), pp. 83–84.
[3] Neil Heller and Thomas Benz, *The Great Tape Debates* (White Plains, NY: Knowledge Industry Publications, Inc., 1987).

costly production studios needed. Nonbroadcast video could and did travel everywhere. Electronic news gathering (ENG) gear enabled nonbroadcast video producers to create programs in the farthest corners of a company's reach. The wilds of an Alaskan oil field, the heat of the Everglades, the remoteness of an underground Utah salt mine—all became studios for nonbroadcast videos.

The ½-Inch Format

In 1976, ½-inch videocassettes were introduced and quickly supplanted ¾-inch in the area of distribution. With almost the same picture quality, ½-inch Beta or VHS tape is half the size, weight, and cost of ¾-inch. A 1987 study found that ½-inch VHS and ¾-inch U-Matic are in a virtual tie for distribution. A 1980 survey indicated that Beta was a distant second, and since that time it has shrunk in use.[4] It is safe to assume that ½-inch VHS will most likely be the nonbroadcast tape distribution method of the future. For now, ¾-inch U-Matic seems safe as the production mainstay.

Other formats are continually being developed and introduced. They include 8mm, Super VHS (SVHS) and digital (D2). While engineers agree that digital video represents the future, it may be some time before the format is widely accepted.

INDUSTRY ACCEPTANCE OF NONBROADCAST TELEVISION

It is hard to pin down the first nonbroadcast entity to operate videotape recorders. It is generally felt that AT&T, the communications giant, was the first to install video equipment. But, it also

---

[4] Judith Tereno Stokes, *The Business of Nonbroadcast Television* (White Plains, NY: Knowledge Industry Publications, Inc., 1988).

seems possible that the first system was a 2-inch Ampex system installed in 1968 at U.S. Steel headquarters in Pittsburgh.

Nonbroadcast television was for many years treated as an unwelcome houseguest by its better known brother, broadcast television. But, as the need for specialized programming has grown and the economic strength of the industry has become apparent, nonbroadcast television has attained prominence. The International Television Association (ITVA), which began in 1975 with 800 members, today has over 8000 members in the U.S. alone. Its 1988 convention drew over 1200 attendees. The industry trade show, Video Expo, attracts thousands of attendees in New York, Los Angeles and other cities. Hundreds of dealer–sponsored equipment shows attract thousands more.

While "downsizing" of some departments and even elimination has occurred, the value of the industry is no longer in dispute. Economic downturns, corporate takeovers, and some genuine managerial ineptness have sidetracked the growth of some nonbroadcast departments.

Today, it is estimated that there are over 49,000 professional nonbroadcast television users spending an estimated $5.5 billion in programming and equipment in the United States alone. By 1995, this figure is expected to climb to over 83,000 users spending an anticipated $12.6 billion.[5]

AUDIENCE ACCEPTANCE OF NONBROADCAST TELEVISION

Audiences readily accepted nonbroadcast television because they were already familiar with broadcast television in their homes. The effectiveness of these early pieces of nonbroadcast equipment soon developed a marketplace that fueled the need to create

---

[5] Stokes, *The Business of Nonbroadcast Television*, pp. 13–15.

equipment, formats and programming specifically designed for nonbroadcast use.

PRESENT USERS OF NONBROADCAST TELEVISION

While some organizations are relative newcomers to the field, others have successfully used nonbroadcast video since its inception 30 years ago. Present users include corporations; hospitals, extended-care facilities and related medical facilities; public and private school systems, colleges, universities and other institutions of higher learning; local and regional cable television systems; satellite distribution companies; government agencies, including branches of the armed services, the National Park Service, national museums and other nonmilitary branches of government; and nonprofit organizations.

While many of these organizations have extensive in-house staffs and facilities, others have small staffs that contract for outside services to produce their programs. In addition to outside production centers that offer video production services, numerous freelancers serve the nonbroadcast video industry.

In addition, the proliferation of nonbroadcast television has created new uses for a familiar medium: narrowcasting, teleconferencing and interactive video.

Narrowcasting

Narrowcasting is the opposite of broadcasting. Broadcasting disseminates programming to anyone with a receiver. Its topics are usually broad-based and often entertainment oriented. Local television stations and the networks are good examples of broadcasting.

Narrowcasting disseminates a program to a specific audience. Narrowcasted programs include training, information and communication for certain specific audiences, such as training a group of machinists or a group of salesmen for an insurance concern. Narrowcasting may be done using a simple VCR and TV set to play tapes on. Or it may involve more elaborate distribution means such as interactive video or teleconferencing.

Teleconferencing

Teleconferencing has experienced a great deal of growth within the past decade. One reason for this expansion is the addition of several competing firms to the field that offer various teleconferencing services. Another is that technology has lowered the cost of the necessary components in teleconferencing, therefore, reducing the cost to the potential user.

Broadcast television blazed the initial trails in satellite use. Beaming news stories from around the globe, a rare occurrence in the late 1960s, has become a commonplace event for local stations and network news, and the proliferation of satellites has increased the number of channels (transponders) available for use.

One form of teleconferencing- videoconferencing- uses the advantages of satellite technology. Videoconferences usually tie together similar groups of people in diverse geographic areas to watch and participate in a discussion held at a central site. Often, the central location provides the video and audio for all the locations and is known as an *uplink*, while the outside locations, referred to as *downlink* sites, can participate by calling on phone lines and talking "live" on the air during the broadcast. This form of videoconferencing is also known as business television. Two-way videoconferencing provides fully interactive audio and video between two locations that resembles face-to-face meetings.

It is estimated that 21% of all colleges and universities produce at least one videoconference a year; during the same period a little over 10% of all primary and secondary schools have participated in such an event.[6]

---

[6] Stokes, *The Business of Nonbroadcast Television*, pp. 69-72.

While videoconferencing has been limited to the facilities cost for the business sector, corporate television has in the last five years been expanding into this area at a greater pace. The lower cost coupled with the need to expand training and communication services within organizations has fueled a dramatic rise in satellite teleconferencing use.

In 1987, 14% of all businesses and industry produced a video-conference.[7] Most organizations try teleconferencing in an ad hoc manner. That is, the facilities, technology and consultants are arranged on a one-time special basis. The occasion may be an address from the CEO, introduction of a new product line or advanced training for a group of employees. Several of these "special events" may be held using downlink locations, such as hotels or other meeting places.

Once it is determined that videoconferencing has worth to a company, a "network" may be built that incorporates permanent installation of receiving dishes on downlink offices' roofs. Then, too, a company may decide to build its production center based on videoconference production. This may include the acquisition of a sending dish and the components necessary to uplink when-ever necessary. This decision is often a costly one, easily running into the millions, and is obviously what prevents many companies from establishing their own business television networks.

However, as will be pointed out in Chapter 3, a number of companies have opted for the establishment of their own networks. It seems that the growth of teleconferencing will be strong in the coming years.

Interactive Video

Interactive video allows the viewer to work with or "interact" with the video program he or she is watching. Generally, a viewer

---

[7] Stokes, *The Business of Nonbroadcast Television*, p. 45.

watches a training program and, at certain preplanned intervals, a menu appears and requests the viewer's participation. The request may come in the form of a test, a review or a query to determine if the participant wants further information. By answering the question correctly, either by entering the response on a computer terminal or touching the screen, the program advances to the next section. Again, the process may repeat itself.

The PC-Based System

There are currently two basic systems for interactive video. The first utilizes a PC (personal computer) and tape recorder. The PC follows the program and advances or stops the tape as needed. The VCR is programmed with various training or informational segments. If after presenting the information, the viewer needs more training on the same subject, the PC will repeat the previous programmed module or go on to a related module.

This system allows flexibility and is cost-effective. However, shuttling the tape via VCR can be time-consuming and eventually wears out the tape. Another system is more efficient but carries a stiffer price tag.

The Videodisc System

The videodisc system uses a laser disc with all programming and testing material concentrated on the disc itself. (See Figure 2.1.) The disc can carry considerably more programming and information than a tape and it can be used constantly with little wear and tear. It is, however, expensive to manufacture and current equipment does not allow for program changes.

The videodisc is used predominantly in education, training and point-of-sale applications. It is estimated that currently 8.5% of all corporate video users are using interactive videodisc systems.

Figure 2.1: Programming an Interactive Videodisc

Courtesy Reliance Electric.

While interactive video as a means of training and point-of-sale is a worthwhile concept, the cost and inflexibility inherent in disc production will continue to thwart its mass use.

CASE STUDIES IN NONBROADCAST TELEVISION

The success of nonbroadcast television hinges on the people who produce it. As the technology changes and the need for more communication and training grows, the need for quality communications professionals also grows.

Later chapters describe actual jobs in nonbroadcast television. The following three case studies of nonbroadcast video professionals describe who they are, where they came from, and where they see the profession going. Picture yourself in their shoes—in their departments. Then turn to Chapter 9 to discover the many job titles, responsibilities, career ladders and other pertinent information about nonbroadcast television.

Eugene Kutina
Director of Corporate Video
Cigna Insurance Corporation
Philadelphia, PA

Video operations at Cigna are conducted in an elaborate facility based at the home operations in Philadelphia and fed to a large network of field offices. Cigna, five years ago, was formed by the merger of INA (Insurers of North America) and Connecticut General insurance companies. The department proved its worth by playing an important role in dispelling rumors by disseminating information about the merger to employees. As Cigna is currently preparing to move to new headquarters, a state-of-the-art facility, the department is evolving in the direction of information processing and dissemination.

Personal History

Gene started his career in the Air Force as a training instructor with audiovisual emphasis. Upon completion of his obligation, he enrolled at Kent State University in Instructional Technology. He received his bachelor's degree and taught high school for two years before re-enrolling at Kent and completing his master's degree, again in Instructional Technology.

His first job after receiving his M.A. was again in government. This time, he was in instructional training and rehabilitation with the Veteran's Administration. After two years, he moved to Roadway Services, a freight transportation company. He started as a training administrator and soon evolved into video instructor for the growing concern. Starting as a one-person operation with a closet TV studio, Gene built up the department in the next 10 years to include four people, much equipment and a large studio. They were charged with the task of producing several tapes a year as well as administering several teleconferences.

He started at Cigna as the assistant director of corporate video and, in three years, was promoted to director of the department.

Primary Video Applications

Currently, the direction of the department is changing from a production center that only distributes programs to several hundred locations via cassette tape to include a local area network (LAN) system. The Cigna LAN will be a delivery system that combines teleconferencing, a bidirectional multi-point cable and microwave system that includes 128 potential channels of live and taped programming, information management, passive electronics and video bulletin boards. This state-of-the-art system will interconnect all the information gathering systems within the corporation and be available in a highly efficient and usable format.

As Gene states, "The cost justification of simply getting rid of much of the paper—memos, announcements, manuals, files— makes our system a necessary part of the future of the corporation."

People/Equipment/Facilities

The Cigna corporate video department consists of seven people augmented by many freelance production personnel. Because of Cigna's location in downtown Philadelphia, the availability of freelancers with quality skills is abundant. The video center is primarily a 1-inch facility.

View of Nonbroadcast Video

Gene feels that the days of nonbroadcast video professionals being involved primarily with the production and distribution of nonbroadcast programs are over. As he puts it, "We're moving into a whole new area of processing and distribution of information. The boundaries between the various mediums are blurring as technology advances. Video, computers, graphics, slides, overheads—all are merging. And as they are being produced, they are used. The nonbroadcast video professional can no longer be just a production person who learns management skills. He's a gatherer and distributor of information. And in this sense, it's a whole new field."

Scott Carlberg
Management Communications Coordinator
Phillips Petroleum
Bartlesville, OK

Phillips Petroleum is one of the energy companies that has undergone radical changes in both mission and size in recent years. Since the "boom" years brought on by the oil embargo, Phillips has watched its stock plummet due to the dropping price of oil and two attempted hostile takeovers, which depleted cash reserves.

From an employee base in 1981 of 37,000, its size has shrunk to a base of 21,000. The concentration of personnel is almost totally in the oil and chemical industries.

Personal History

Scott started his career at Western Illinois University with a degree in Communications with television production emphasis. Obtaining a graduate assistantship, he stayed at WIU and obtained a master's degree, also in television. After much searching and sending of resumes, he received two offers at almost the same time. One was a sales position with an electronics manufacturer, while the other was as a producer/director with Phillips.

He made the decision to take the job for Phillips and moved to Bartlesville, OK, in June of 1975. His goal was to make useful corporate television programs for Phillips and to build an internal nonbroadcast communications network. During the early 1980s his department grew until it required an annual operating budget of over $700,000. Along with that growth, Scott became the department's supervisor.

But his greatest challenge lies ahead. As the company began to cut back, the video department had to shrink accordingly, while providing the necessary communications services. Scott has been able to reduce the department's annual operating budget to $475,000, while still adding and marketing additional video capabilities.

Due to this success, Scott was moved in July of 1988 into the position of management communications coordinator with direct access to top management.

Primary Video Applications

In addition to training, the department is responsible for product promotion, including gasoline and motor oil via trade shows and customer call tapes, employee and management communications, safety, community awareness, as well as a biweekly 5- to 10-minute news program. The video network has over 150 distribution points nationwide with an additional 10 sites throughout the world.

People/Equipment/Facilities

There are currently six people in the Phillips corporate video department. Headed by a supervisor of video and engineering, the department consists of a senior and two junior producer/directors, a production assistant and a distribution/control room assistant.

Boasting $1.75 million in equipment, the facility features CMX 340X computer editing (soon to be upgraded to the more versatile 3400), digital video effects, a Grass Valley 100 video switcher, a Dubner character generator, three HL Hitachi video cameras and one Ikegami camera. The department has enough portable remote equipment to record with all four units in different locations at the same time, which, apparently, has been necessary on occasion. They both master record and edit on 1-inch VCRs except for field shoots where they utilize 3/4-inch and occasionally 1-inch VCRs. They distribute mainly on 1/2-inch VHS with some locations receiving 3/4-inch distribution.

View of Nonbroadcast Video

Although Scott liked his video supervisor duties, he feels the job of management communications coordinator is a "rewarding extension of practical corporate communications." He still maintains a close relationship with the video department.

Regarding nonbroadcast television, he states that "I love the challenge. If you want to get into nonbroadcast, I suggest you learn business management. You can always learn the specific hardware later. I also feel strongly that writing skills are important to the industry."

Having conducted several interviews as a manager and given a considerable amount of advice to job seekers, Scott suggests, "When you send a resume reel, don't send anything you coproduced. Send only things that you were solely responsible for. If you're applying for a writer's position, you should have at least five different scripts to show potential employers.

"The same thing applies in applying for video production positions. Have a number of different kinds of programs on your reel to show your versatility."

David Phillips
Producer/Director
Ernst & Whinney
Cleveland, OH

The video department at Ernst & Whinney, one of the big eight accounting firms, is less than five years old. With over 28,000 people located in 115 domestic and 80 international locations, the need for quality video communications became evident. The two-person department operates out-of-house for production facilities and talent and produces a variety of programming.

Personal History

Dave started gathering his television experience while working on a B.S. in Communications at Ohio State University. One day a professor wrote a phone number on the board and stated that "these people are looking for someone to help out in video."

Dave called and soon landed a part-time videographer position with Lazarus Department Stores of Columbus, OH. At the time, the department had a camera, recorder, a closet TV studio and hired a part-time writer.

Proving his mettle, Dave was hired full-time as manager of studio operations. However, a mild recession cut the budget and he soon had little to do. He left to work on cars with his brother, but he later plunged full-time into getting another position in the field.

His hard work was rewarded with a position as a video specialist in a two-person operation at the May Company Department Stores in Cleveland, OH. He credits his involvement with ITVA as an active member and chapter treasurer for providing him with the information needed to get this and his next two positions.

Dave stayed at the May Company for three years and then sought a chance to expand his responsibilities. He did so by interviewing for and gaining a position with Robinson Memorial, a regional hospital. As part of a general expansion, the hospital was installing satellite and closed-circuit operations when Dave was hired as media manager.

After three years, the hospital's fortunes began to ebb. Rather than stagnate in the position, Dave interviewed at Ernst & Whinney and was selected over 43 other applicants.

Primary Video Applications

The department produces proposal work and support programs, training tapes, employee communications, benefits program information and recordings of partner meetings and other gatherings. (See Figure 2.2.)

Figure 2.2: Dave Phillips Preparing a Studio Shoot for a News Program

People/Equipment/Facilities

There are two people in the department. The department has only a small amount of video playback equipment. All programs are created out-of-house by contracting with production houses and freelance personnel. Last year the budget for producing over 50 programs was $400,000.

View of Nonbroadcast Television

Dave calls nonbroadcast television "an exciting field. There's a certain rush working with people to create programs. If it ever loses its appeal to me, I'll quit. Right now, I can't wait to get to work.

"My advice to those looking for a job is to encourage you *not* to specialize in just acquiring television skills. Acquire writing skills, develop your overall communications techniques, work on your personal relations with others and, by all means, pick up management techniques."

3
The Nonbroadcast Television Marketplace

This chapter describes the fields that comprise the nonbroad-cast video marketplace. At the start of each section is an overview of the specific field. Following each overview is a section entitled **Possible Contacts.** This section is designed to get you thinking specifically about each field in terms of your immediate market-place. You will be able to zero in on names of people and com-panies, in order to start putting together a contact list of leads to start your job search.

By using the questions in the contacts section you will be able to systematically "walk through" the exact marketplace you are currently in or would like to be in.

There are a number of fields that make up the nonbroadcast television marketplace. (Appendix 3.A at the end of this chapter contains brief descriptions of jobs in the nonbroadcast television market. More detailed descriptions of positions with explanations of concomitant career paths are covered in Chapter 8.) While surveys have broken the industry into three, four and even five separate fields, the actual number varies according to the size of the parameters used. As the purpose of this book is not to shrink the scope of your search, but rather to assist you in widening it, I have identified nine separate areas of nonbroadcast television: education, corporate, medical/health, cable, satellite, advertising and public relations, production house, freelance and consumer.

EDUCATION

Educators were one of the first groups to see the potential in using television for communication other than entertainment. In the late 1950s, they began by scrounging up discarded and often antiquated equipment from local television stations. With a few grants, they began producing instructional and educational programs for clearly defined audiences, for example, eleventh grade biology, first year art appreciation, and adult education.

Distribution

At first, the programs were shown on the local National Educational Television station (now known as the Public Broadcasting Service or PBS). Eventually, because of the explosion in need and the quantity of programs, educational programming expanded into nonbroadcast avenues.

Many colleges and larger school districts have installed radio frequency (RF) systems that operate as mini-cable stations within campus classroom buildings. These systems operate on channels assigned by the institution's instructional television departments and operate exactly like a cable television system.

For example, Channel K may be programmed to run first-year legal programs at 10:00 A.M., 1:00 P.M. and 7:00 P.M. Channel A may be running advanced painting techniques for art classes every hour, starting at 9:00 A.M. Still another channel, B, might be showing the vivisection of a frog at 9:00 A.M., 11:00 A.M., 1:00 P.M., 3:00 P.M., 5:00 P.M. and 7:00 P.M. for biology students.

Another popular method of distribution pioneered in the mid-1960s and very much in use today utilizes the carrier bands on the local PBS station. By scrambling the signal, the Instructional Television Frequency System (ITFS) beams programming to area school systems where the signals can be unscrambled for viewing in the classroom.

In both of these methods, programs are distributed in a "shot-gun" approach. That is, large audiences view specially designed training tapes at specifically assigned times. The program cannot be stopped or replayed. Also, the ability to *narrowcast* (see Chapter 2) to one or two people or just one specific class became desirable in education.

Flexibility in Distribution

The smaller tape formats, 3/4-inch U-Matic and eventually 1/2-inch Beta and VHS, offered more flexibility. The school's audiovisual department could hook up a VCR and TV on a movable cart and wheel them into individual classrooms for viewing. Also, study carrels (specially designed study bays) equipped with monitors were added to libraries or Learning Resource Centers (LRC) for individual student viewing of tapes.

Program Design

Flexibility in distribution encouraged educators to design their own programs tailored to the specific needs of their courses. Audiovisual departments (which, at first, only included technicians or communications assistants charged with the responsibilities of operating the playback equipment) were requested to design instructional television programming for individual courses. Thus, audiovisual instructional designers were no longer only technicians but became creative artists who could examine an educational task, define the problem, select the proper media, design software (programming) to achieve an objective and then produce the program for use in the classroom.

Colleges and high schools soon found many applications for instructional television. With increased demand came the need for specialists versed in the operation and preparation of this new, powerful medium. Library and audiovisual departments began instructional television divisions that produced and distributed programs. As the cost of equipment decreased and the number of instructional applications increased, the need for television specialists, versed in production, distribution, and instructional design, expanded.

The Audiovisual or Instructional Television Department

The basic college-level audiovisual or instructional television (ITV) department often is an adjunct to the library. It designs various materials necessary to impact the educational process. This includes graphics such as charts and graphs, audiotapes, slides, slide-tape, photography, multi-image, overhead transparencies and video production. The department consists of one or more people who work directly with instructors and recommend, assist, and design the instructional materials. Most high schools have similar setups with at least one audiovisual person.

Scope of TV in Education

Elementary and Secondary Schools

A survey commissioned by the Corporation for Public Broadcasting (CPB) and the National Center for Education Statistics (NCES) focused on how far instructional television has entered the elementary and secondary school classroom. The 1982–83 *School Utilization Study* found that during the 1982–83 school year 71% of all teachers had ITV available, and of that group 54% used it. The study showed that the equipment manufacturers had done their homework well— over 75% of all schools had one or more VCRs available for use in 1983, up from 33% in 1977.[1]

---

[1] Judith Tereno Stokes, *The Business of Nonbroadcast Television* (White Plains, NY: Knowledge Industry Publications, Inc., 1988), pp. 59-60.

In 1985, a survey by Quality Education Data (QED) found that 79% of all schools had video for instruction. A 1986-87 phone survey moved the figure up to 90%. The norm for schools is one VCR for every 10 classrooms, according to QED's *Video Purchasing Patterns in Schools, May 1986.*[2]

Colleges and Universities

At the college level, the 1984-85 CPB-NCES survey found that videocassettes or videodiscs were available via the AV or ITV department in 90% of the institutions. The Stokes study, *The Business of Nonbroadcast Television,* found that almost 95% of all colleges produced programs in-house, a figure roughly the same for all educational users surveyed in the study.

The Business of Nonbroadcast Television also found that nearly 85% of reporting educational users had a television studio for producing instructional videos. Colleges and universities were found to be more likely to have video facilities than secondary schools. However, of all educational institutions, 97% owned video cameras; over 86% owned sophisticated electronic editing equipment for the production of programs.[3] Obviously, if they have the equipment, then they have the need for people to operate it for the creation of quality instructional programming.

Applications in Education

Colleges' and universities' ITV departments often have a variety of services and personnel available. The department's producer looks at a particular problem within the educational process

---

[2] Jeanne Hayes, ed., *Video Purchasing Patterns in Schools, May 1986* (Princeton, NJ: Quality Education Data, Inc., 1987).
[3] Stokes, *The Business of Nonbroadcast Television,* pp. 67-69.

and decides on the course of action and medium to use in order to obtain the best results. For example, a biology professor may have a great deal of visual information on genetic engineering, but may be at a loss as to how to present it. Discussion with a media producer may reveal that the best medium to use would be video. This is not always the case, however. The producer may sense that the professor would be more comfortable with a slide program, or perhaps, due to budget and time limitations, multiple screened overhead projections might be more appropriate.

There are a multitude of video services that schools and colleges can provide. At the basic level are the simple recording and playback of classroom instruction. This is particularly useful in departments where students can learn new skills by watching themselves on videotape. For example, a speech student can learn a great deal about the mechanics of speaking by watching a videotape of his/her performance.

Sometimes a basic video recording is made of a special outside speaker for use at a later date. Medical and dental classes often use video to explore students' techniques as well as to teach procedures.

More elaborate programs can be designed to meet specific needs. A professor may have a module or group of discussions in which several different visuals are necessary. An instructional television program can be made that could control the information provided to the student and guarantee the impact of certain statements within the module. Chemistry courses might contain 50 or 60 separate 20-minute modules to explain the various elements and parts of molecular structures.

When special speakers or noted authorities work with a particular class, the discussions are often recorded for use in other classes. Off-the-shelf programs that are produced in tandem with textbooks are often purchased to enhance the learning process. In this way, students can enhance their understanding by viewing programs directly related to their coursework.

In many schools the communications department produces student news programs that communicate to the educational audience while giving students practical experience in television.

Training is the primary use of ITV. A survey titled *Instructional Technology in Higher Education* for CPB and NCES reported in May 1986 that colleges and universities also used ITV for student counseling, community outreach programs and promotion and recruitment.[4] A familiar example can be seen on televised football games. The half-time programs that promote the competing colleges are usually produced by the ITV departments.

Some colleges are producing adult learning coursework modules that are mailed to the student along with a text. Students read the assignments, watch the tape and are tested periodically with an exam they send back to the institution for grading. Such courses are accredited and allow universities to reach home-bound, hospitalized, or simply unavailable-for-class students, who wish to pursue higher learning and training. A 1984 CPB-NCES survey found that 32% of all colleges and universities offered such "telecourses"; 57% of them offered the courses on prerecorded videocassettes and 59% aired them on public television.[5]

Many large educational institutions have made a commitment to instructional television. In such circumstances, large staffs, elaborate studios and sophisticated field equipment are the norm.

Careers in Education

Job descriptions and career ladders are extensively covered in Chapter 9. What follows is intended to give you an understanding of what the positions are and how they interrelate.

Instructional Television Department Managers

Basically, department managers are responsible for the overall direction of their departments. They hire and fire personnel, make

---

[4] Stokes, *The Business of Nonbroadcast Television*, pp. 57–60.
[5] Stokes, *The Business of Nonbroadcast Television*, pp. 60–62.

equipment purchases and work in tandem with the administration to make certain that overall goals are in line with the institution's mission. Manager/directors must be leaders who can inspire a diverse group of troops to tackle the educational problems identified by faculty. They must set priorities and initiate follow-up to be certain programs are being developed on time and within budget.

Sometimes department managers are responsible for funding, which may include the obtaining of grants. They work with faculty, set the overall tone for the department and assign individual programs to certain producers. They prepare the budget and keep the staff on target and within budget.

The pay scale generally ranges from $25,000 to $35,000 per year. Some top colleges will pay up to $45,000 for this position. Often, advanced degrees are required. Most colleges would like at least an M.A. in Communications or Instructional Design. Smaller colleges will demand only a bachelor's degree, but the pay is commensurately less. You may be allowed to add to your education during your tenure. Education is the one area in which advanced degrees are continually rewarded by promotions, responsibilities and remuneration.

Instructional Television/Audiovisual Producers

Similar to the position of instructional designer, producers have responsibilities for overall production, from the idea to execution, of an instructional program. Most producers wear many hats in terms of audiovisual materials. They may develop a slide-tape program, an audiotape series, graphics including maps and charts, photo layouts and entire videotape programs. Most medium to large colleges have instructional television departments and may have as many as one to five IT/AV producers.

Producers must be able to work with faculty and administration as well as the production crew. They must have unusual foresight to see what is needed to complete a given project and then, by working with others, have those things ready when needed. Working with artists, production assistants, editors, writers, talent and clients, while keeping an eye on budget and time, can make the job of producer exciting.

Good producers enjoy high degrees of job satisfaction, and their skills should allow them to move into industry or broadcast television. Pay scales start around $18,000 and stretch, according to experience, education and tenure, to $25,000 per year.

Producers looking for advancement generally have an eye on the department manager's job or a similar producer job in another area of nonbroadcast television.

Writers

Writers work with the client and the producer to formulate the program. A program may be rewritten many times to accommodate both producer and client. Research is a big part of this position, and writers must learn the technical language before they can translate it into an instructional medium. Word processing skills and an understanding of both AV and television production are necessary. The ability to work with many different people is also a must in this position. Pay scales run from $12,000 to $15,000. Although the job of producer can be the next step, writers tend to stay in their element and may turn to another nonbroadcast television field for growth.

Production Assistants

General production assistants range from student assistants to part-time and full-time personnel. In addition to distribution assignments (distributing media materials to classrooms), the position includes production assignments like operation of studio and remote location equipment, setting of lighting, staging, mike placement and recording. The ability to work with others while learning quickly is important.

Working as a production assistant is a good introduction to nonbroadcast television that allows a person to sample the different parts of television production and distribution, but is not usually designed for long-term employment since production assistants are not frequently promoted. Good production assistants usually move upward with another company. Except for those PAs who show success in certain key production elements like editing, writing, or producing, you will not get rich as a production assistant. This entry-level job pays minimum wage to $10,000 per annum.

Technicians/Engineers

Technicians/engineers are responsible for the technical health of the equipment. Most ITV technicians must be able to repair AV as well as video equipment.

Technicians/engineers like to problem-solve. They must also like to work alone and enjoy reading technical manuals. In an industry where equipment changes quickly, they must work hard just to stay current. Often, they advise the department head as to which equipment is deteriorating and recommend replacements. Television system design is becoming a part of this job.

Salaries for audiovisual and video technicians at small facilities range from $12,000 to $15,000. Engineers earn from $18,000 to $25,000. A complicated system could push the pay scale upward.

Media Specialists

Media specialists look at the various educational problems presented and determine which medium is appropriate to use. They help design programs and are often the people who set up audiovisual presentations using slides, audiotape, overhead projectors and graphics.

This position is found in all high schools and most major colleges. It is not unusual for school systems to employ several media specialists, as media in general and television in particular have had a large impact on the educational process.

Annual salaries range from $10,000 to $13,000 for small school systems and high schools. In large school systems, junior colleges and universities, media specialists can earn $20,000 to $23,000 per year.

Developing Contacts in Education

What colleges, universities and junior or community colleges are in your area? Do they have libraries, media centers or learning resource centers? Do they utilize video in those areas? To what extent? Who is in charge? Who is responsible for instructional television for the institution? Who is the department head, producer, technician?

Are there communications departments within those same institutions? Do they teach the use of video in any courses? What equipment do they have? Who is in charge of the courses and equipment?

How about the athletic departments? Are they on local cable or broadcast television? Do the schools package the games or is it done by another organization? What personnel do they use? Where do they come from? Who makes decisions?

Do local school districts and high schools make use of video? Do they record speeches? Do they make use of the educational access channels available to them on local cable channels? Who is the ITV decision maker?

Are there other organizations that use video as a part of their instructional process? These might include museums, foundations, nonprofit associations and clubs. Give them a call. Even if they have not used video yet, they may be planning to.

If you are a novice, you may think that calling organizations to learn about their uses of video might be a case of "the blind leading the blind." It can be if you have no experience at all in video. But, if you have some experience, I have met many people who started with a germ of an idea that they developed into major video projects.

Employment Prospects

The ITVA surveys of 1986 and 1987 point out that educational institutions have smaller budgets than nonbroadcast television departments in other fields. This is reflected in the salaries they pay. However, they do offer plenty of job security, peak and off-peak work schedules and unusually good benefits packages. State and public pay scales are public records, and most advertisements indicate the pay range up front.

While school districts continue to operate under tight budget constraints (usually voter approved), colleges and universities openly compete with each other for students. Because of that, they are more likely to upgrade and expand their television facilities. Also, more higher learning institutions are offering coursework in television. This means that equipment will be purchased for use in classes. Many ITV departments have alliances with communications courses.

Overall, the outlook for expanded use of nonbroadcast television in the educational setting and therefore the employment of nonbroadcast personnel is good. The reason is simple. We are in the middle of another baby boom. Parents are more educated than the parents of the last baby boom generation. They realize that education is of great importance to their children's future success. As the school-age population increases, school districts will be forced to provide more money for education, and a greater ratio of students are expected to go on to college and advanced degrees. More students, more education, more money for education, more money for educational tools!

Still, the unfortunate truth is that nonbroadcast jobs in education will continue to pay less than comparable jobs in industry.

CORPORATE (INDUSTRIAL) TELEVISION

Corporate television is the fastest growing segment of non-broadcast video.

Today, companies that never dreamed of producing a television program are becoming ravenous video users. In 1974, the first Brush report on the corporate video industry indicated that there were more than 300 corporations spending over $48.5 million for nonbroadcast video.[6] The following year ITVA started with 800 members.

In 1980, *Video in the 80s* reported that corporate video usage had increased to over 13,500 users spending an estimated $660 million. In 1988, *The Business of Nonbroadcast Television* estimated 23,000 users spending an estimated $3.3 billion. By 1995, corporate television users are expected to reach 40,000 spending over $7.5 billion![7] Certainly, corporate video is exploding.

Corporations have turned to video to facilitate their communications for the following reasons:

• **Consistent Message.** Management has absolute control over the message. The same message can be sent to every employee in each location.

• **Flexibility.** The message can be disseminated immediately and is easily shown on the various playback units conveniently located throughout the corporation. Everyone knows how to operate a VCR. The program can also be updated and changed by electronic editing.

• **Cost.** A major factor in any profit-making endeavor is cost. Nonbroadcast video saves time and therefore money by getting the message to the field faster and without the need for travel.

---

[6] Judith M. and Douglas P. Brush, *Private Television Communications: The New Directions* (Cold Spring, NY: HI Press, 1986).
[7] Stokes, *The Business of Nonbroadcast Television*, pp. 14–17.

A new product or service can be introduced without meetings, travel, entertainment or time-consuming in-person presentations.

• **Credibility.** In a nation where television news is consistently given the highest marks for credibility, corporate video information is easily absorbed by employees. Rumors can be eradicated quickly by the use of employee news programs.

The 1986 Brush Report indicated that the top 10 corporate television applications for the future, ranked by nonbroadcast professionals, will be news programs, employee information, employee orientation, employee benefits, management development, management communications, supervisory training, community relations, annual reports/meetings and point-of-sale programs. In the survey, the most common applications for corporate video were for job training and employee benefits information.[8] In recent years corporate video has been used extensively as a management/ employee communications vehicle. (See Figure 3.1.) The change can be attributed to a management philosophy of improving communications with employees. Video is the vanguard in this role. That is one reason corporate video is the hottest area in nonbroadcast television.

Careers in Corporate Television

There are three basic areas in corporate television: production personnel, management and technicians. Chapter 9 will provide a more detailed breakdown of job titles in these areas.

Production Personnel

All production personnel must have a good working knowledge of television production. Although some corporations have intern-

---

[8] Brush, *Private Television Communications: The New Directions*, p. 17.

Figure 3.1: Filming a Corporate News Program

ships and production assistant positions to provide on-the-job training, experience is usually necessary to obtain entry-level positions. Production assistants are the lowest-paid personnel. Sometimes they earn a little more than their educational counterparts, in the range of $10,000 to $12,000 a year.

Other production personnel with definable skills (for example, audio engineer, cameraperson or gaffer) are paid based on the size of the department, tenure with the firm, level of flexibility and experience (corporate video people often wear many hats), size of the firm, location of the facility (people are paid more in New York City, than, say, Oregon) and knowledge of the firm's industry. For a definitive look at corporate salaries, there are several surveys available, which are listed in Appendix B at the back of this book. Average annual production salaries in corporate television range from $15,000 to $28,000.

Management

In corporate video, the one-person shop was the norm, but has become less common. In these cases, these management/production/technical positions average an annual salary of approximately $25,000.

Some one-person shops result from reducing the size of the video department, either as a result of economic constraints or because it has been decided, for any number of reasons, to shrink the department to the barest of essentials. For example, the video department of a bank chain in a small town in Mississippi was reduced to a one-person shop when a merger was proposed. The lonely manager was not happy about his plight. He feared the worst—that he would also be laid off. He called me in hopes of networking and finding another position.

Salaries of media center directors and corporate video supervisors are based on the amount and type of responsibilities they have, the number of people they manage, their relative standing and tenure within the organization and all of the contingencies listed under production personnel. With these disparities kept in mind, video supervisor positions garner an annual salary between $25,000 and $35,000. Directors, responsible for departments including but not restricted to television, earn a salary of $35,000 to $45,000. A video-only director of a single department, however, would earn about 20% to 30% less.

Technicians/Engineers

Technicians are responsible for maintenance, system engineering and upkeep. Their jobs are similar to those of technicians/engineers in the educational field, but since the corporate sector is profit-oriented, the equipment tends to be more current. The demand for engineers is increasing. Pay is currently from $21,000 to $25,000 per year.

Contacts in Corporate Television

Professional Organizations

Career advancement through contacts and personal growth are the prime advantages of belonging to the ITVA, the professional organization for the corporate video communicator. National, regional, and local meetings and workshops are held for beginners, intermediate and advanced television production personnel. The organization publishes annual salary and compensation surveys, operates a job hotline, publishes a membership directory (with over 10,000 entries), publishes newsletters, holds an annual awards festival and national convention and offers a multitude of other benefits to members.

ITVA has advanced the career of many people in the nonbroadcast video community. I urge you to get involved with any of the video professional organizations such as ITVA, IABC (International Association of Business Communicators), PRSA (Public

Relations Society of America) or AMI (Association of Multi-Image). See Appendix C at the back of this book for further information on these and other organizations.

Participation with colleagues is a good way to build a track record and gain experience. Involvement can go beyond being just a member or meeting attender. Serve on committees, help publish newsletters, direct dinners and awards banquets, speak at workshops, do anything that will help you to meet and work with other people in this industry. The people working for local or regional organizations are often the first to know what is happening where and which companies are expanding their video departments.

Research Companies in Your Area

Besides the many local and national organizations, whose membership directories should be the first on your list of potential contacts, you should identify the large- and medium-sized companies in your area. Are the headquarters or divisions of large companies located in your area? These companies are most likely to have existing video departments.

Do any of these companies use video for sales training, employee training or customer information? Do they use video in employee communications or for customer point-of-purchase sales? Many retailers have found point-of-purchase video to be valuable. Who in your area uses it? Where is it produced? Who is in charge? A good place to start your research is in your local library. The business section should have directories of companies that contain this kind of information.

How do the local utility companies (gas, electric, phone) use video? What departments use it, and who is in charge of the operation?

Just because a corporation does not presently use video does not mean that someone does not see its potential and understand the need. You should contact all department heads who might consider using video for the benefits it would bring to the company. Your call or visit may be just the thing that gets the ball rolling.

As the Brushes stated in their fourth survey:

> Once it was said that only big companies or large organizations could use video. Video then was a "big buck" item in anyone's budget . . .

> What is apparent is that size has no longer anything to do with whether or not an organization is using private (non-broadcast) television. The primary reason that any organization uses video is because it does an effective job in communications and/or training. The same kind of problems are faced by an organization with 1,500 members or employees in four or five locations as a company with 100,000 spread throughout the world.[9]

In other words, virtually every company in your area has a potential need for video and the expertise you have. Even smaller, privately held concerns have video needs that can be tapped into. All it takes is time, effort and the ability to reach the right person. Use the Yellow Pages, State Manufacturing Directories and Chamber of Commerce information to help add to your contact list. Any friend or relative who works for the company can provide a valuable introduction to the "right" person within the organization.

Employment Outlook

Corporate video prospects are very good. In fact, this area represents the greatest growth in nonbroadcast television. You should be aware of the fact that many companies are now supple-

---

[9] Brush, *Private Television Communications: The New Directions*, pp. 52-54.

menting their full-time staffs with part-time personnel and free-lancers. This makes it a more volatile marketplace. As a freelancer or part-time employee, an employer can see how you will work out in the organization. If you can prove your merit as a freelancer or part-time employee, an offer of full-time employment may follow.

CABLE

Cable television (CATV) was initially used as a master antenna television (MATV) service for areas that either had poor reception and/or were sparsely populated. There was little planning for local, regional or satellite program production and distribution. All that changed when the Federal Communications Commission (FCC) decreed that CATV stations with over 3500 subscribers were required to produce programming for local communities. Such programming would be provided on channels known as local origination (LO) and would be produced locally.

According to figures published by the National Cable Television Association (NCTA) in 1985, 75,000 people were employed in cable franchises that have been awarded in almost 18,500 communities. Presently, some 3700 CATV stations produce LO programming. There are cable systems in every state and in every major market. A number of the systems are owned by MSOs (multiple system operators). There are also over 6700 individual cable systems.

Local origination provides an outlet for the community to program television for itself. Most systems designate at least one channel for LO. A few have many, such as Manhattan Cable (NY), which has over 20 channels with programming available for anyone who can hold a video camera.

Many CATV stations operate more than one LO channel. One might be an educational channel for local educational institutions. It will often show programs such as sporting events, graduations, student-produced news shows and telecourses.

Religious channels provide nonstop programming for various local and some regional and national denominations. Civic channels are usually the domain of City Hall. Many communities now broadcast their council meetings as a part of regular "town hall on-the-air" programming. Civic fairs, festivals, election campaigning and even Fourth of July fireworks have been known to be staples of such programming.

Careers in Cable

CATV stations are not the place to get rich. Even the NCTA points out that while top jobs in cable can reach the $100,000 annual mark, most jobs are in the lower ranges from $12,000 to $25,000.[10] They do, however, afford hands-on opportunities to learn production, particularly in some larger stations that schedule production classes to teach potential LO users. As LO is a profit drain, full-time production personnel are kept to a minimum. Production management is often skeletal with many of the duties centering on scheduling.

Cable television, because of the number of operating cable companies and the generally low wages (thereby leading to high turnover in the lower positions), is a good place to gain experience. It can turn into a career as well.

When I was a freshman at Ohio University, cable television was necessary for television reception in rural areas such as Athens, OH, home of Ohio University. The cable company wanted a part-time person to spell its only production person/quasi-engineer. I took all the hours the regular engineer did not want. That meant I worked Sundays from 12:00 A.M. to 6:00 P.M., the Saturday

---

[10] A good sourcebook on cable is *Making It in Cable TV* by Joshua Sapan (GD-Perigee Books, Putnam Publishing Group, 1984). Specific occupations are detailed in a booklet entitled *Careers in Cable* (National Cable Television Association, 1984).

night 10:00 P.M. to midnight show, and any other time he wanted off. My duties were to make certain the weather dial camera worked (it rotated in a circle) and to play 16mm films at designated times.

The Saturday night show was when we really let our hair down and played films backwards, took the weather camera off, did remotes (as far as the camera would reach) and played records. All of this was in the studio, a 10-by-10-foot hut next to the antenna on the highest hill five miles out of town. It was not much, but I was in television! In addition, the experience opened the door for other part-time and internship assignments for me.

For a friend of mine, cable television provided the full-time engineering job she had always wanted. She started as an audiovisual technician in high school. While at college, where she earned a two-year associates' degree, she worked in the instructional television department and learned about television electronics. Her experiences led to an offer with a local cable firm and she has been their chief engineer ever since. The CATV station and her responsibilities have grown immeasurably.

Production Personnel

The responsibilities of production personnel in cable television are the same as those in corporate and educational video. Minimum wage is the starting point for most production jobs in cable TV. Salaries are generally 10% to 15% less than the same jobs in corporate or broadcast television.

Contacts in Cable

There are over 30 different cable companies programming a variety of LO channels in Manhattan, NY. There are 12 in Cleveland, OH, four in Columbus, OH, 12 in Chicago, IL. If more than one cable company programs in your area, find out who they are and what they do. This information can provide you with leads. Who is in charge of the various LO channels in your community? A good place to begin looking for this information is your local newspaper listing of programming for cable television channels. Other resources are the *Television and Cable Fact Book* (published by Warren Publishing in Washington, DC) and *Broadcasting/Cablecasting Yearbook* (published by Broadcasting Publications in Washington, DC), which contain listings of cable companies by geographic areas.

On the other side of the franchise award, what local governments, school districts, church groups and medical organizations are currently programming on cable? Who is in charge of getting these programs on the cable? What civic and governmental organizations could benefit from the LO channels, but through lack of knowledge of the medium or cable company have not availed themselves of the opportunity? Which person in the organization could make a decision regarding using the LO channel for the group's benefit?

Employment Outlook

The prospects in cable television are generally good. The number of independent companies, however, is decreasing due to combining of individual cable systems by MSOs. It is still unclear if this will have any effect on employment prospects. More than 50% of the country is now wired for cable, so start-up operations are rare.

SATELLITE PRODUCTION

Satellite production is one of the areas that crosses over into other areas of nonbroadcast video. Many organizations, including colleges, corporations and nonprofit organizations, have put together satellite networks that provide programming that is transmitted on a sending dish, known as an *uplink*, to a satellite *bird*, which then disseminates the information to several receiving stations known as *downlinks*. Video is often one-way to the receiving sites and two-way via phone lines to all sites. At present, it is estimated that there are over 50 satellite networks that transmit programming on a monthly and often weekly basis. And virtually every month, the number increases.

Satellite services include the organizations that produce programming (e.g., ESPN, HBO, American Management Association, American Bar Association, American Health Network) and the distribution companies, which sell and engineer the services (e.g., VideoStar, Bonneville and Private Satellite Network). They coordinate the sites, provide engineering services and set up the uplink and downlink stations.

Business Television via Satellite Distribution

Corporations and institutions have learned to use satellite distribution of programs, known as "business television," to their advantage. For example, the Kodak Business Television Network (KBTV) broadcasts 25 hours of programming each month to more than 60 downlink office sites located throughout the United States, Mexico and Canada. This programming carries information and training for the 20 operating units of Kodak as well as employee news and management communications.

The KBTV network also broadcasts programs for pickup by the general public. For example, three or four times a year, the program "Techniques of the Masters" is uplinked so that schools and other institutions of higher learning can pick up and record it for later use. The program deals with famous photographers. By showing their work and interviewing them, it is hoped that aspiring photography students will be able to learn from the best.

Business television's influence has grown. Recently, KBTV produced the first "Business TV Today," a forum to exchange information and ideas among all business television network users.

The Help-You-Sell real estate company delivers sales training, communications, motivational messages and real estate agent recruitment programming to over 30 sites. Based in Salt Lake City, UT, this franchise organization uses business television to enhance the effectiveness of its communications to achieve an edge in today's competitive market.

The Automotive Satellite Television Network (ASTN), based in Dallas, TX, broadcasts several hundred hours of programming to over 3200 downlink sites. Dealing primarily with the automotive aftermarket, ASTN is one of the largest business television networks of its kind.

Satellite Video Conferencing and Networking

Satellite video conferencing remains one of the hot new technological tools for business and industry. One-way "live" and two-way audio is one of the configurations used. Compressed video and other variations are used, as well.

Federal Express uses its business television network for a variety of training and communications needs. Recently the network was used as a marketing tool. Marshall Loeb, managing editor of *Fortune Magazine,* presided over a satellite videoconference that had over 200 downlinks worldwide. Billed as "What's Ahead for Business After the Election," the conference, produced at the NBC studios in New York, attracted several thousand viewers.

Hospitals are using business television to disseminate information regarding medicine and health techniques. Computerland is cross-networking with Domino's Pizza on topics of mutual interest, like building a business and desktop publishing. Domino's network is centered at their 25 distribution center sites to receive approximately 15 hours of programming per month. Computerland's network is presently at 80 sites, with 20 more planned to be operational by late 1989. The network carries programming on training, product introductions, employee news and information, press conferences and production information from outside vendors.

Clearly, with the age of information processing and distribution upon us, satellite videoconferencing and business television networks are at the cutting edge of technology.

Careers in Satellite

In the last five years, the use of satellite distribution has exploded. Associations and companies that provide programming need a variety of production and engineering personnel.

Satellite distribution companies have openings in sales and engineering. As the number of satellites increases, so will the demand for qualified personnel who have experience in this field. As many colleges, universities and cable companies use satellite services, they are excellent starting points to gain experience in this field.

Contacts in Satellite

The International Teleconferencing Association

The International Teleconferencing Association (ITCA) is a professional organization that can help you in this field. Their annual exposition draws over 2000 attendees and is a great place to meet people and learn about the field. The 1989 Convention, held in Washington, DC, was the largest to date. Additional guides to garnering contacts include the *Video Register & Teleconferencing Resources Directory*, the *Telespan* newsletter, and *Business Television* magazine (see Bibliography for further information).

Local Companies

Find out what companies in your area use satellite distribution (A tip-off is the big dish sitting behind or on top of their buildings.) What do they send or receive via the "bird?" Is satellite distribution internally controlled or do they depend on other companies for service? What companies are involved? What hotels are involved in satellite networking? Who operates the service and what do they offer?

Where does the programming come from for satellite channels like ESPN or CNN? Is any of it local? What about local athletic teams? Who puts them on the "bird?" Who puts together the production for the game? As sports, home-shopping and religious satellite channels grow, so do competition and the need for programming. If you see anything that is locally produced, find out who did it. (Hint: read the credits when you watch the show.)

Satellite distribution is growing. The latest Brush report concluded, "All indications are that the entire field of videoconferencing—both permanent one-way network systems and dedicated two-way systems—are in for a period of explosive growth over the next several years."[11]

Future Prospects

The employment outlook in satellite production is very good. An explosion in satellite communication is just beginning. In recent years the number of satellite companies has decreased due to mergers and acquisitions. The consolidated companies have more money and less competition, so watch for growth in this segment of the industry in the 1990s.

HEALTH AND MEDICAL INSTITUTIONS

Hospitals, fueled by the need for quality instruction and communications, have turned to nonbroadcast television for their

---

[11] Brush, *Private Television Communications: The New Directions*, pp. 147–152.

needs. Because of their size and resources, health organization-based video has become one of the fastest growing specialities in non-broadcast video. Some facilities do everything from shooting actual surgery to working with doctors to produce programs. They may also run in-room patient network channels and create, write, produce, and market nursing and medical personnel training programs. Some health organizations also operate satellite networks designed to communicate medical knowledge.

Careers in Health Television

Because of the similarities among medical, corporate and educational video, many of the career tracks are similar.

Contacts in Health and Medical Services

Professional Organizations

The Health Sciences Communications Association (HESCA) was formed for professionals who are involved in the applications of television to health education. HESCA is located at 6105 Lindell Blvd., St. Louis, MO 63112 (314-725-4722). This diverse group covers all areas in the medical field and has a section known as MEDPRO (for Medical Production and Distribution) that seeks to improve the qualities of all health programming. In addition to publishing the bimonthly *Feedback* newsletter and the quarterly *Journal of Biocommunications*, HESCA operates an annual convention.

The Association of Biomedical Communications Directors (ABCD) has 87 members and a budget of less than $25,000. It is more diverse in its membership with professionals coming from allied fields such as veterinary, dental, nursing, and pharmaceutical. The Association of Biomedical Communications Directors is located at the Louisiana State University Medical Center, Box 33932,

Shreveport, LA 71130 (318-674-5260). Dennis A. Pernotto, Ph.D., is the director.

Hospitals

What hospitals are in your area? How do they use video? Are any of them "teaching" hospitals? Do they have education centers? If so, education centers are frequently users of video.

Do any of the hospitals program on the cable LO channels? Do they contribute to the satellite health channels? What are their medical specialties? Often, when a hospital is considered a leader in a specialty, it will use television production and distribution facilities to disseminate information to other hospitals.

Other Medical Resources

What other medical organizations are in your area? Mental Health boards, the American Red Cross and the American Cancer Society often use nonbroadcast video to communicate. Who is in charge of these organizations and, more important, who is in charge of making the decisions regarding video? There may already be a video unit in place.

Medical insurers, such as Blue Cross, and health maintenance organizations (HMOs) have found video to be helpful for their communications needs. Who is in charge of the HMO communications departments? Which departments are using video, which should be using video?

Local Health and Medical Institutions

Once again, the telephone book and the local library are good sources of information. The medical section of local business directories should give you enough information to start your search.

Future Prospects

The job outlook in nonbroadcast video for the health and medical field is good. The economics of healthcare in this country are undergoing change and restructuring. Generally, the profit-based hospitals and HMOs have a stronger financial base than other medical institutions. Therefore, they provide more extensive video services.

ADVERTISING AND PUBLIC RELATIONS

While the making of commercials and public relations programs is often handled by a separate department, many PR and advertising agencies have recognized their clients' needs to develop in-house communications programs. Also, as technology advances, nonbroadcast- and broadcast-quality television have converged. This means that the broadcast departments of agencies are now handling nonbroadcast video projects as well. They now have a need for people with nonbroadcast television experience to market, design and produce nonbroadcast programs.

Contacts in Advertising and Public Relations

Professional Associations

A membership in the local chapter of PRSA (Public Relations Society of America), IABC (International Association of Business Communicators) or the local press club or ad club would come in handy. All are looking for new members, so find out who is in charge and go to a few meetings. Advertising agencies and public relations firms are listed locally, so start contacting them. While they may not have video equipment, they do employ "creative" types who write and create programs, and account representatives who sell and service the various clients. By working in these organizations, you will make contacts that can help you obtain a job in an organization that does have video equipment.

PRODUCTION HOUSES

In order to support the production needs of nonbroadcast clients who have elected not to build their own internal facilities, production houses offer a variety of services. Sometimes, nonbroadcast facilities use outside production houses for specialized services to add to their programs. Services include basic single camera, advanced multi-camera, studio and location recording, complex post–production services, including computer editing, graphics design, programming of diverse digital video effects and audio mixing and sweetening.

Production houses usually specialize in certain services. Some are known as "post houses," which have several editing bays and expensive digital effects equipment. They may own animation gear that few single nonbroadcast users could afford. Others are known for their quality remote electronic field production (EFP) work. Still others concentrate on audio and specialize in the creation of musical scores and sound tracks for nonbroadcast productions.

Careers in Production Houses

Production houses are organized the same way most nonbroadcast television departments are. Unlike nonbroadcast departments, however, they must turn a profit; therefore their staffing is usually thin and their abilities to grow and ebb are directly related to the economy of the clients they serve. When business is good, they staff up. Recessions, however, often hit them quickly and hard.

Positions available in most production houses include production assistants, videographers, editors, character generator operators, master control operators, directors, producers, technical directors, gaffers, sales people, accountants and writers. Salaries for these jobs generally range from $15,000 to $30,000 per year.

While some entry-level positions are available, advanced positions, like computer editor, require qualified candidates with prior experience on specific equipment. The houses offer employees an unending variety of programs and challenges. Truly gifted individuals are rewarded by the outside client's desire to return due to that person's creative and interpersonal skills. The abilities to take on a lot of work and work with a variety of people while being a problem solver are required for success with production houses.

In the last five years there has been a trend toward using outside production houses for nonbroadcast productions. This has come at a time when equipment, facilities, and personnel costs are at an all-time high. It has come as a result of companies realizing that they do not necessarily need to tie up their profits buying video capital equipment when they can purchase quality production services and thereby save overhead.

Some corporations and educational institutions have found it a lucrative practice to also provide out-of-house production services. In this way, they are able to provide video services for their main client, their company, and add to their bottom line profits from their outside clients. (See Figure 3.2.)

Contacts in Production Houses

A simple look through the local yellow pages or any of the trade publications' production services guides will reveal companies catering to the needs and desires of the local or regional video community. Production houses often belong to the professional organizations. These organizations' membership rosters will contain their names and locations.

Employment Prospects

The future looks very good for production houses. Many organizations that use nonbroadcast video have found it cost-

Figure 3.2: AVID Productions' Control Room. AVID
Sometimes Functions as a Production House for
Out-of-company Clients

effective to own minimal playback equipment and utilize the
services of production houses. Because equipment changes so
quickly, many corporations and nonprofit organizations cannot
afford the latest "new" production tool. But production houses
can and *do* offer the latest production equipment.

FREELANCERS

Freelancers provide a growing pool of talent that offers a
variety of production services to several different clients. While
freelancing started due to a lack of jobs for people with advanced
skills, freelancing is now being embraced by people who want to
experience the freedom of this entrepreneurial field.

Today, there are more freelancers operating than at any previous time. Freelancers offer a variety of services: writing, shooting, production assisting, editing, directing, planning, audio mixing,
and talent (both on and off air). (See Figure 3.3.)

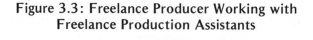

Figure 3.3: Freelance Producer Working with
Freelance Production Assistants

While this avenue is not for the beginner, many tenured non-broadcast people have found freelancing to their liking. The decision to freelance, however, is a decision to go into business for oneself. You have to develop a client base and keep your skills honed and refined. And if you are going to go into business, you must learn everything it takes to run a business. It means you have to be "business conscious" and keep track of your expenses, billing procedures, and tax accounting information. Some practical business courses would be useful if you plan to take this route.

A freelancer must have something to offer to someone who is willing to purchase it. Be certain your skills are marketable before embarking on such a career move. Some typical freelance positions include writer, videographer, producer, director, editor, production assistant, lighting director, character generator operator, teleprompter operator, gaffer and grip. Many freelancers offer two or more skills to distinguish themselves from the rest of the industry.

Freelancers are paid either by the hour or by the job. A typical salary is $20 to $25 per hour or $150 to $250 per day.

Contacts

Freelancers develop contacts in the same ways as in other segments of the nonbroadcast television industry. The library and the local telephone directory are good places to start. Contacts from previous full-time or freelance jobs can be important. Some freelancers use their skills to obtain a full-time job. Some local ITVA chapters have made an attempt to list jobs for freelancers.

Future Prospects

Freelance work in nonbroadcast television is definitely increasing. Companies often find it easier (and cheaper) to deal with freelancers than to hire a full-time employee.

CONSUMER SERVICES

As equipment has become less expensive and easier to use, hobbyists and entrepreneurs with a more than passing interest in nonbroadcast video are developing their talents into businesses. These include services, such as videotaping weddings, religious events, parties, legal depositions, underground equipment placement and meeting documentation. Some of these companies are operated out of homes, in small offices or storefronts. Some include post-production facilities geared to the very small nonbroadcast user. One of my favorite images is the post-production facility run by an individual who has a 1-inch editing bay in the basement of his house!

While some of us tend to ignore these industries, they are answering a need that many consumers have. Single camera wedding shoots now cost from $300 to $1000. A firm that tapes a wedding with three cameras, a portable truck that houses a switcher, a VCR, a director and engineer and post-produces the program later might charge $3000 to $5000 per wedding.

An insurance adjuster developed his video hobby into a full-scale fire insurance videotaping service. He records valuables and properties for later claim justification and assists with fire department inquiries to determine the cause of suspicious fires by recording the fire and consequent damage.

Another person started a video deposition service for lawyers who could not get expert witnesses to commit to testifying due to the uncertainty of the trial length.

The courts have allowed videotaped expert testimony and, because more liability cases use expert witnesses, there has been a significant increase in video deposition services. Many "experts" testify in several cases each year and cannot make each trial date, thus the use of video. Also, for the defendant or plaintiff to pay the expenses and daily rate for the expert to "wait his turn" on the witness stand would not be cost-effective and would impair the defendant's right to a fair and speedy trial. Therefore, video depositions are on the increase.

Besides expert testimony, depositions have been taped when witnesses or plaintiffs have moved and cannot make the specific trial dates. While one side may pose the questions, the other side is given equal opportunity.

An insurance executive built an entire company around videotaping automobile accidents and fires. The tapes are used as evidence in hearings and court cases. This "actual scene of the crime" videotaping has allowed determination of responsibility in accident and arson cases.

Businesses like these represent a new arena of opportunity for those interested in entering the nonbroadcast video field. The success is totally dependent on your ability to fulfill a need. While the initial cash outlay might be minimal, the eventual rewards depend on your ability to provide a service someone will pay for, at an affordable cost. Your marketing expertise will then determine the rest.

CONCLUSION

In times good and bad, due to changing technologies, new services, and decreasing hardware costs, nonbroadcast video has continued to grow.

Presently, nonbroadcast television includes all the associations, institutions, corporations and government agencies that seek to "narrowcast" to select audiences. Nonbroadcast job opportunities exist in education, corporations, medical, services cable, satellite, advertising and public relations, out-of-house production firms, freelancers and consumer areas.

When looking for a position in nonbroadcast television, you must start with a list of potential contacts. Once you have scoured your geographical marketplace and defined your contact list, you are ready to start marketing your most important asset.

And that, of course, is YOU!

APPENDIX 3.A: JOB DESCRIPTIONS

Videographer: operates the camera, selects shots, records shots to tape.

Editor: Mixes various shots with graphics, mixes audio sources.

Production Assistant: Assists in all phases of production.

Lighting Director: In charge of setting lights.

Audio Technician: In charge of recording audio on remote and studio shoots.

Master Control Technician: In charge of cueing videotapes and setting up sources like slides and shading of cameras for editing or recording process. Functions as an assistant to either live recording or edit sessions.

Floor Manager: In charge of the studio during studio shoots. Takes orders from director.

Director: In charge of directing the overall program. Responsible for sets, props, actors. Rehearses actors and cameras for actual shooting. Responsible for on-location and studio shooting.

Producer: Responsible for the overall concept and eventual direction of a program. May select talent, director, editor, crew. Either is the client or interfaces with the client. Responsible for budget and overall goals being met by the program.

Assistant Producer: Assists producer in overall producing of programs. Usually does all the detail work for the producer.

Executive Producer: Works with producer for overall direction of production. Responsible primarily for financial details and deadlines. Will work with client to assure that objectives of program are being met.

Production Coordinator: Assists in scheduling and budgeting of all audiovisual productions. Assists producers in any number of ways to help complete productions. Responsibilities include writing, set design, location assistance, setting of pre-production meetings and follow-through of post-production.

Administrative Assistant: Responsible for the clerical side of the nonbroadcast video department. Includes word processing, library coordination and administration, teleprompter preparation and financial bookkeeping for the department.

Media Technician: Overall assistant knowledgeable about the technical workings of most of the video equipment. Performs minor maintenance and sets up equipment, studios, conference rooms and audiovisual setups.

Engineer: Responsible for the technical operation and overall quality of the equipment. Designs systems and monitors equipment with engineering gear to insure proper operation. Trains personnel on setup and operation of systems. Responsible for equipment maintenance.

Writer: Takes content of program and develops a script treatment and script to meet the objectives set for the program. Involved in rewriting as necessary.

Audiovisual Specialist: Primarily involved with audiovisual equipment, such as the setup and operation of slide, overhead and motion picture projectors, audio recorders, slide-tape programs and training or conference room setup. May design some smaller audiovisual productions. Usually, involvement in video is just one aspect of this job.

Graphic Artist: Responsible for preparation of graphics, slides or prints needed in the production of a program.

Character Generator Operator: Operates character generator and related electronic equipment to produce electronic visuals for productions. May include three-dimensional animation.

Supervisor: Usually supervises a video department or a section of a media center. Coordinates all scheduling of productions, equipment and personnel. Supervises personnel and coordinates budgets.

Manager: Responsible for the overall direction of department or departments. Is responsible for budgeting, hiring and firing of personnel, planning of new technology and interfacing with clients to provide quality service. Markets department's services and looks for new ways to assist clients via nonbroadcast video. May also be responsible for other media-related departments.

Instructional Designer: May formulate ideas for program and is responsible for the design of program to meet specific educational objectives. Surveys audience to assess needs and designs program accordingly.

Makeup Artist: Responsible for makeup and hairstyling for talent in a production. May include costume selection.

Talent: On or off camera, is responsible for saying the lines from the script and creating the overall impression necessary to convey the message of the program. Nonbroadcast video utilizes professional and amateur actors.

Sales/Marketing: Associated with either vendor or outside production and/or duplication facility for the purpose of selling services. Equipment vendor salespeople tend to be technician-oriented.

4
Looking for a Job in Video

Any job search or quest for upward movement begins with an assessment of your qualifications and background. That is, what in your work history can directly benefit you, benefit the employer and help you to do a good job in the position you are seeking? Before you look for a new position, you must take stock of what you have and what you need in order to make a move.

If you are currently in television, the task requires you to take a hard look at yourself, much as a prospective employer would. This enables you to see the deficiencies in your background. You can then add the skills needed to round out your experience. If the deficiencies are not germane to the direction your career is taking, then you can prepare to explain them to a prospective employer.

If, on the other hand, you are new to the television industry getting that first job with no real practical experience may seem impossible.

But first, a few points for you to consider:

TIME

The personnel industry estimates that every $10,000 of salary you intend to make in your new job will require four to six weeks of constant, full-time searching.[1] This means that finding a $10,000 a year position will take approximately a month to a month and a half of full-time work to find and start. A manager

---

[1] Robert Half, *The Robert Half Way to Get Hired in Today's Job Market* (NY: Rawson, Wade, 1981), pp. 41-43.

looking for a $40,000 a year position should anticipate a four- to six-month search.

BEGINNING THE SEARCH

In September 1971, armed with not one, but two degrees in television (I was of the school that if ONE was good, TWO had to be better), I left the security of campus life and pursued my dream of a career in television. I knew I would make it. After all, that was what college was all about: to prepare me to enter the job market I had selected and embark upon my life's career.

By November, I was selling uniform rentals for a dry-cleaning establishment.

While I eventually made my way into the wonderful world of nonbroadcast television, I made an astounding discovery along the way.

No one . . . neither the professors nor I . . . had prepared me to find a job. Not only did I not know how to look for a job, but I had not adequately provided myself with marketable skills. Nor did I know how to present those skills to a prospective employer.

Before you can embark on the hunt, you must take stock of yourself.

WHAT DO YOU WANT TO DO?

It's estimated by psychologists that 80% of all currently employed people hate what they do.[2] Incredibly, they spend two-thirds of their waking hours working at that job.

Before you even picked up this book, you should have spent a great deal of time thinking about what it is you want to do in

[2] Robert Levering, *A Great Place to Work: What Makes Some Employers So Good and Most So Bad* (NY: Random House, 1988).

life. Your family, peers and friends are probably telling you to "get a job, dress right, settle down" and basically live like they do. They lead secure and fairly conservative lives.

There are other people, however, who seem to risk everything to do what THEY want to do, not what other people want them to do. These people do fail from time to time. Often they do not have approval for the way in which they run their lives from their elders or even peers. But, they are doing what THEY want to do.

Most of us tend to fall somewhere in between. But the ability to do what you want to do for a living lies within you. Make no mistake: video is a tough market to break into, and changing jobs later within the industry does not get easier.

What do you want to do with your life? What are your goals? You can achieve anything, if you truly want to. But are you prepared to take risks to achieve what you want in life? What will you do to attain your goals?

There has always been a shortage of bright, creative people in television. Nonbroadcast television, much more than broadcast, affords you the opportunity to reach very far, but it requires the abilities to listen, learn and practice.

For example, if you want to be a writer, then you should spend long hours writing and rewriting letters, stories, memos, scripts, training materials, technical articles– everything. Good writers, as any famous author will tell you, are not born. They learn their skills through practice, practice and more practice. Furthermore, there are no guarantees as to whether they will be successful. How many children have taken piano lessons, and yet there is only one Horowitz!

I have two close friends who spent hours before and after school, during weekends and late at night practicing skating routines on the ice rink. Both went to competitions and enjoyed some success, but neither became stars.

And yet, their eyes light up when they talk of their exploits on ice. They had a dream, aimed for it, did their best and are better for it. They will always have that experience. They always tried.

The point is this: You might not become the Cecil B. DeMille of video, but if you make a commitment and give it your all, you will make a contribution that is tangible. And the rest of the industry will be better for it. If you are going to try, give it all you have. And, like my friends who skated their little hearts out, your name may never be in lights, but you will be better for it. And you will join the 20% who really enjoy getting up in the morning and going to work.[3]

To be successful in nonbroadcast video, you must be willing to stretch and take that extra chance. You must put forth energy with no guarantee of success. But if you make a concerted effort and try, it can never be taken away from you.

WHAT SKILLS DO YOU OFFER A PROSPECTIVE EMPLOYER?

What useful marketable skills do you have that would make an employer sit up, take notice and want to hire you?

If you are currently employed in the television industry, take stock of your experiences and be honest about your potential benefits and shortcomings. Imagine yourself sitting across the desk from someone with exactly your qualifications. Does that person have the background to insure success?

What has that person done in his/her past that indicates success? How does that success translate into potential for you? Will the potential employee fit in at your facility and with your people? Where has the person failed? Why? Has the individual learned anything from failure or is he/she apt to make the same mistakes again?

How can he/she help you? Will you be saving time, money, and so on? How much time will you have to spend training the

---

[3] Levering, *A Great Place to Work: What Makes Some Employers So Good and Most So Bad*, p. xx.

new employee? Has the person made it crystal clear that you, the employer, will receive benefits by making him/her a part of your team?

Notice that the emphasis is on what the candidate can do for the employer, not on what the employer can do for the prospective employee. All too often, job applicants consider only what the job will do for them, and not what they can do for the job. The production facility you are looking at may have the latest in computer editors, digital effects, state-of-the-art graphics systems and an impressive physical plant, but what are YOU bringing to the job that will benefit the EMPLOYER?

IF YOU DO NOT HAVE EXPERIENCE, GO GET IT

You should do everything that is possible to acquire the necessary skills and experience.

Lest you think that only entry-level people have experience deficiencies, consider this: Bill worked for a Fortune 500 company for a decade. He was the manager of a large corporate television facility when his company threw him a curve. In the belief that moving an employee to an unrelated function broadened his managerial skills, the company moved Bill to the advertising department. He soon quit.

Freelance Experience

Bill became a freelancer. And here was where he gained a great learning experience. As pointed out in Chapter 3, a freelancer is an independent business person who sells, promotes, does the job, then bills, collects, pays his own taxes and, hopefully, makes a profit.

Bill did not make a profit as a freelance producer. He had plenty of talent, but did not have the resources to obtain equipment. However, he did learn how to run a nonbroadcast video business. His experience became critically important when he joined a large independent post-production facility. His previous experience enabled him to survey the marketplace and invest in up-to-date equipment. He was responsible for turning the facility into a profitable enterprise.

If you are new to the industry the need for experience will probably be all you hear from employers. And it may seem impossible for you to gain experience when literally thousands of others are trying to do the same, and the opportunities for gaining it seem very limited.

To gain the necessary experience it is essential that you work around, in, near or with a video, graphics, photographic, motion picture, audiovisual or advertising-related facility. If you are campus-bound, there are a number of places to volunteer your time and services while gathering valuable experience. Sometimes, volunteer positions work their way into full- or part-time work. They are a great way to learn while allowing the employer to see how you work out.

Temporary Employment

A variation on this situation has worked well for experienced people who are between positions or unemployed. Executive search professionals have used this technique successfully in industries that experience high turnover.

If you are unemployed and interview for a position you know you are qualified for, but the employer is reluctant to commit, offer to fill in as a temporary employee for a trial period, perhaps two to four weeks. The benefit of such a move to the employer is that he/she can get *some* production out of the position immediately, while ascertaining your worth to the organization.

The benefit to you is that you are working and receiving a wage for something you are familiar with. You have also effectively moved your resume to the top of the heap by filling the job, at least, for the time being. Even if the employer and you do not come to terms, you will have gained another practical experience.

In a world where temporary services abound and in an industry where freelancing has become commonplace, this scenerio takes place more times than you might think. Recruiters with extensive experience in this method (for example, Management Recruiters International, Inc.) report a placement success rate in over 70% of such cases.

If you still consider this an odd way to gain employment, consider that most nonbroadcast supervisors prefer to offer positions to freelancers they have worked with before. They know what those people can do, because they have worked with them in the past.

Volunteer Experience

For the inexperienced, hanging around and offering to help out can work. (See Figure 4.1.) Maria Keckan, chief operating officer of Cinecraft Productions, Inc., a midwest-based production house, explains how she got her first job in medical video:

> I worked as an intern at a broadcast station. I was a production assistant for 80 one-minute medical spots to be run on network television. My job included holding cue cards, rewriting script copy, patting the talent's forehead with powder, timing segments, logging tape numbers, and anything else a gofer normally does (like running for coffee and soda). When the 80 spots were completed, so was my job, and although I applied for a full-time, permanent position of directing the nightly news, I didn't get it.
>
> I'd always had a strong interest in medicine. In fact I had started out in college with the intentions of becoming a physical therapist, though my direction changed with my first elective film course. But, now, with college graduation almost upon me, medicine seemed to call me once again. One of my last courses was a business marketing course in which I had to select five companies and interview their marketing personnel. I selected hospitals for my project. I learned then that Fairview

Figure 4.1: Volunteer Experience Led to a Career in
Medical Video for Maria Keckan

Photo courtesy of Maria Keckan, Bill Moga and Joe Puthoff.

General Hospital was the only local hospital producing
and marketing educational videotapes for national distribution. I knew immediately that that was where I
wanted to work.

I called personnel and asked for the name of the
person in charge of the audiovisual department. I then
called the woman in charge, Pat Lehman, and asked if I
could come in and just talk to her. I told her I was very
interested in her department and what they were doing
because they were unique. At the time she had an
assistant producer and one secretary working for her.
She explained there were no job openings and she did
not foresee being able to hire anyone in the near future.
asked if I could still just talk with her and see the
department. She agreed and we set up an appointment.

When I arrived I was surprised to find no cameras
or audiovisual equipment. Pat explained to me that all
production was done in a television studio, in fact she
was going to be producing something that night at a
local station I'd never visited. I asked if I could go along
and watch. She reluctantly agreed. During that evening I

helped her unpack and arrange artwork and made myself as helpful as I could without being obnoxious. When we had a chance to talk I told her one of my strengths in school had been scriptwriting. She thought that over for a moment, then asked me if I might be interested in freelance writing a script on electrical safety for hospitals. I told her I'd love to (while my mind said, what are you, crazy, Maria, you know little about hospitals and nothing about electricity!). Needless to say, in two weeks time, working day and night through Christmas vacation, I learned everything there was to know about electrical safety in hospitals and wrote a 30-minute script on the subject.

I made an appointment with Pat Lehman and took the script in to present to her. I handed it to her and was about to leave when she said, "Sit down, I'll read it now." I sat in front of her desk and watched her read it, slowly, page by page, and I thought my heart was going to jump out of my chest, it was beating so hard. I was certain that she would think my amateur attempt at the professional world of nursing education was inadequate; maybe she would even laugh. She sat there composing her thoughts when she was done and then told me that this was the best script she had ever read and that she would figure out a way to hire me. I started as a secretary and within six months I was writer and full-time producer. I worked there for eight years until the opportunity to buy Cinecraft Productions came along.

Finding Experience on Campus

If you are still on campus, there are many places that offer you the chance to gain practical nonbroadcast experience.

The School's Educational TV Station

Many large universities have a PBS station on campus that uses student help. Sometimes, the station is operated separately from the academic curriculum area of television or communications. That separation should not prevent you from seeking employment there. Receptionists, secretaries and gofers for these stations have moved into production positions and eventually management. It is a golden opportunity you cannot afford to miss.

The College's Media Center

While I was in college 10 other students and I started "pushing audiovisual and video carts" around campus. Eight of us currently have highly successful careers in video. Often understaffed and always needing people willing to learn how to set up various types of equipment, media centers offer jack-of-all-trades type experience. You can learn a lot about equipment and how various materials are prepared for certain media. It allows you to discover exactly what you like and want to do in the industry.

College Radio Stations

Students often forget that television without the visuals is radio. The fact is that many tasks and situations that occur in radio or audio production are similar to video. Editing, recording, post-production, writing, rehearsing, engineering—all are areas in which radio can give you solid, practical experience.

The Campus Newspaper or Yearbook

Before radio and TV, newspapers were the dominant medium. Early radio and television writers came from journalism. Moreover, the ability to write is the foundation on which we build most non-broadcast television productions. A former student of mine took a job in my department as a secretary, not because she wanted to be a secretary, but because she wanted to utilize her writing skills for video. Previously, her experience included being entertainment editor for the campus newspaper. She made the transition to television writing very easily, eventually writing some scripts, and now works as a production assistant for a large government contractor.

Internships and Independent Study

Internships are a great way to gain experience. Because the student works at the organization's location, he/she gains far more than simple video skills. The student learns, firsthand, how American industry operates and gains an appreciation for decision making and an insight into how and why decisions are made. The intern learns the etiquette and dress of the business world and sometimes is hired by the company after the internship ends. If not, he/she at least gained a solid work experience that will mean a lot to other employers.

Internships are often arranged by the college department. The best ones are usually snapped up and spoken for early. So start contacting your professors and counselors and asking for leads six months to a year *before* you want to begin your internship.

But let me give you a golden hint: **Find your own**. There are still too many students and too few corporations and other organizations offering internships. I suggest following the career search procedures explained in this book, only use them for an internship. If nothing else, it will be great practice.

Start with a contact list. Determine where you want the internship to be located. This is usually the site of your college or your home town. If your college town was like my first college town, namely small, then you may have to look to the next larger town.

Write down names of possible internships you hear about from other students and professors. Be aware of corporations and institutions in town and, if you attend one of the professional organizations as a student member, write down the names of the people you meet and contact them later.

It never hurts to take the initiative when you are seeking an internship. For example, Bradley was in my senior corporate television class at John Carroll University. He was one of the better students and seemed very interested in nonbroadcast video. He, like so many other students, had never heard of the industry before taking the class and was generally enthusiastic about the field. He was excited by production, demonstrated his ability to take command and direct productions, and did extra work that involved watching other corporation's programs (we had a tape library) and visiting nonbroadcast television departments.

Halfway through the course I gave my internship speech and explained how it was a good way to get that all-important first "experience" that employers insist on. And, at break, Bradley approached me.

"Do you offer internships where you work?" he asked.

"Why sure," I replied.

"Okay. So how about me?" he asked. Put on the spot, I mumbled my agreement. He quickly produced his internship form for the fall semester. He was one of the best interns we ever had.

But internships can be unsuccessful, so let me offer some advice, based on my experience as an employer of interns:

- If you are going to intern, be enthusiastic about it.
- Know something about the company before you go. If nothing else, seek out a prior intern from the organization and ask about the job.
- Be realistic about what an internship is. It is a practical experience. You are not about to become a producer overnight.
- You can learn the equipment while on the job. But, it helps to understand the concepts of video production before you start. There are several good books out on television production; you may have one in your production class.
- Chances are, you may not know a lot about nonbroadcast video before you intern. Do yourself and your potential internship a favor and read up on the industry.

- If the company providing the internship should ask you to come in early, before the internship begins, to learn the ropes, take it as coming with the territory and do it.
- Ask the organization's contact if there is any production, post-production or special event coming up that you can attend to help out and get a "feel" for things. It shows that you are interested and may provide an exceptional experience.
- And, if you really feel that you would rather intern at a "real" broadcast station rather than a nonbroadcast facility, wait for that internship. Interning at what you feel is a second-choice experience will do you no good.

Do not wait for your internship to gain the experience you will need to compete in the job market. A variety of experiences broadens your background and makes you more marketable. Other experiences may allow you to gain an even "better" internship. It most definitely will help you beyond your first job.

THE GEOGRAPHICAL DEBATE

"To move or not to move first and try to look from afar," that is the question. None of the job search "experts" can agree on whether looking for a job in Denver while still living in Toledo or picking up the bags and moving first and then looking is better. I have known people who have done it both ways.

A local market in which to job hunt, however, makes life much easier, so I suggest you conduct your initial search in the geographical location you are living in now. If you are in college but are thinking of moving to another area to seek your fame and fortune, be advised that you have reduced your chances of getting a job while you are residing outside that location. If you intend to move to San Francisco, or Atlanta, or Boston or Poughkeepsie, NY, I suggest you move there first and then begin your job hunt.

The reason for lack of success in conducting a long-distance search is twofold: one, there are usually local candidates available with credentials similar to yours. Usually, employers will save themselves the cost of flying you in for the interview and possible relocation expenses by choosing someone local. And second, new employees require most employers to invest orientation and training time and, therefore, they want people to stay with them a reasonable length of time. The desire to change locations based mainly on the climate or whether the surf is up instead of job experience and opportunity indicates to an employer that you may not be around long enough for the company to gain any real benefit from hiring you. Should it become known that you are exploring a certain job market due to your desire to live in a particular locale rather than your desire to advance in your career, your job offers will be slim.

Whether you move first or search from afar, remember that a lot of preplanning and contact work can be done on the phone and by mail.

CAREER ENHANCEMENT

Even if you are no longer starting your career, experience still remains the key to getting that next job. Look upon your career as a journey. And any successful journey needs a road map to show how to get where you are going.

Look at the next step you want to take. Ask yourself, what are the credentials of the person who is filling that and similar positions. What background and what special skills does he/she need to perform the job? If you need technical skills like engineering, then you should do things that will enhance your knowledge in that area. If you need production skills, like directing, then concentrate on the managerial skills that successful directors have. A producer's job requires planning, accounting, negotiations and considerable business acumen. If that is your goal, then plan on gaining knowledge in those areas.

Where to Gain Skills

Necessary skills can be obtained by going back to school for accounting, business, or data processing courses, for example, and on-the-job training. Nonbroadcast television is a team sport, and most members are glad to help one another learn the ropes.

If you cannot pick up the skills needed in-house, then try outside your workplace. Networking with others outside your current business environment enables you to broaden your horizons. I have known several editors who acquired their CMX (and other editing systems) knowledge by moonlighting at other facilities during off-hours. I have known cameramen who have had lighting gaffers show them the ropes so they could use what they learn in the field.

Professional workshops and conferences (e.g., Video Expo, COMMTEX, SIGGRAPH, the ITVA National Conference, ITVA Regional and Local Workshops, IABC Workshops and Seminars[4]) are good places for intermediate and advanced video people to gain additional skills. When I started my career in sales, I took sales courses to give me an edge. Long before I moved into management, I had read dozens of books, attended several seminars and workshops, and had practiced management skills in some volunteer situations. In my case, some of the helping out included serving as committee head for local professional organizations.

Those unpaid experiences do more than just fatten up your resume. They *prepare* you to do the job you want to do. And, when you talk with employers in your search, this preparation will enable you to point out the specific experiences you have had that qualify you.

---

[4] See Appendix C at the back of this book for a list of names and addresses of professional organizations.

A Broad-Based Background Gives You the Edge in
Nonbroadcast Video

Other experiences besides those involving television production equipment will allow you to successfully compete in the job market.

A study by Dr. David Ostroff of the University of Florida asked 99 random nonbroadcast video professionals what experiences they would recommend to people entering or changing jobs in the industry.

Besides the obvious background in video production, these professionals suggested experience or courses in writing and English, business management (dealing with numbers of people and management skills) and computer literacy.

Eighty-five percent of the respondents had college degrees. Forty-seven percent had graduate degrees. But when they were asked what courses and/or experiences had been most useful to them as preparation for their careers in corporate video, they felt that hands-on experiences were virtually equal in importance to on-the-job training, college jobs, internships, English and writing courses.

When asked what they had missed that could enhance someone else's nonbroadcast video career, they indicated a strong need for management and business experiences followed by writing, technical and computer skills.

They suggested that incoming freshmen take courses in video production, writing, business and management and plan on internships as ways to prepare for the nonbroadcast marketplace.[5]

Obviously, there is more to nonbroadcast television than just production. The abilities to work with a number of people (clients, bosses, subordinates, as well as creative, technical and financial workers) and to express oneself via scripts, business memos,

---

[5] David Ostroff, "What Media Professionals Want TV Students to Learn—Now" (University of Florida, 1984).

proposals and reports are necessary. There is an increasing use of computers in our industry. And there is always the need to be able to look at a production and see what works and what does not.

While production skills rank high on the list for those entering or moving within the marketplace, other skills are just as important. Keith Michael McKenney, director of video production for AVID Productions, made it clear to a recent corporate television class at John Carroll University:

> Just having television production skills is not enough to be successful in this industry. You have to know about business. There are a number of courses other than television production you should take. I urge you to take management courses—learn how to work with people. Accounting—not a day goes by when I don't have to read a financial report, prepare one, or send out invoices and keep track of budgets. Computers are here to stay—I may not be completely computer literate, but I'm trying. Look in our control room and you see a number of computer screens. And there are many more of them around for graphics, desktop publishing, word processing and accounting.
>
> Don't think that just learning about how to produce a program is enough. Because, when you enter nonbroadcast, you have to realize that in most organizations, television is not the main business they're in. They are in something else that's the main thrust of the business. It may be making little green motors or producing energy. They don't have to understand your business, but you have to understand theirs so you can succeed. You have to be able to relate what this industry does to them and how it can help them.
>
> You have to learn to talk the language of business to survive.[6]

---

[6] Keith Michael McKenney, Avid Productions, Reliance Electric, in a speech to Communications 420, Corporate Television class at John Carroll University, at his studios in Eastlake, OH, 1986.

NETWORKING

Write all names down to form the basis for a contact list that you will use to start your search. Think about associations you are a part of and meetings you have attended. Networking allows you to be in the right place at the right time, but you need to explore all areas of opportunity. Writing down all the specifics that come to mind will help you begin your career move.

MARKETING YOURSELF WITH THE
FEATURE-ACCOMPLISHMENT-BENEFIT (FAB) APPROACH

It is only by examining your career to date in a clear, objective manner that you will be able to successfully market yourself. And marketing, the selling of yourself, is exactly what you must do.

Once you have a list of contacts, you must learn to present yourself to potential employers. Experience is a must. Presentations using the feature-accomplishment-benefit (FAB) approach will help you gain attention and obtain interviews.

Assessing Your Background

Looking for a job starts first with assessing your background. The next job you are likely to obtain will depend upon what you are qualified to do. The more balanced your background is, the more varied your job search can be and the more doors will open to you. Look upon your background as the means to open up the marketplace. It is your key to the door of the nonbroadcast video marketplace.

Always tell the truth. Honesty is the cornerstone of any job search. If you are ever caught in a lie about your experience or anything you said you could do, your credibility in all other matters will be questioned. Lying is unacceptable.

Scott Carlberg of Phillips Petroleum tells the story of a job candidate who said he could do more than he was capable of.

"We got burned once. We were looking to hire a producer and a guy came in with just a great resume reel. It had a number of programs on it that he had 'coproduced.'

"After he started, we noticed that he just came in and sat around a lot. We got suspicious and started checking his references with more attention to detail.

"It seems whoever he produced the programs with was the real talent behind the material on the reel. This guy didn't know much, but he claimed he knew a lot and was hired on that basis."

While you should never lie about your qualifications, you should be prepared to point out the benefits your qualifications might bring an employer. When looking for a new position, you must emphasize what your accomplishments are and how they are beneficial to potential employers.

Using Your Background

When considering a career move, you have to look at how your background can benefit the boss, the company and the job you are seeking. And you have to be prepared to explain your past. This is where the FAB part of your presentation to an employer comes in. A FEATURE is simply what you have done in your past. Being a cameraperson, editor, director or a department manager is a *feature* of your past.

An ACCOMPLISHMENT is what you did in the job. If you were a cameraperson who shot 60 different productions in 40 locations last year, that is what you accomplished in that position.

The BENEFIT is what the employer can expect to derive by hiring you. In our example, the cameraperson should explain that the amount of production he or she did last year can easily be repeated this year for the new employer. And if a highly productive cameraperson is what the employer is looking for, the cameraperson has enhanced his or her chances greatly by stating features, detailing accomplishments and then stressing the benefits the employer can receive.

The FEATURE—ACCOMPLISHMENT—BENEFIT approach to your background will enable you to "sell" yourself and further your career. Features are simply the things you have done. They may be great and wonderful, but how do they directly benefit the person who may want to hire you? Not unless you quantify your accomplishments and then stress your benefits can an employer start to appreciate your worth.

FAB Presentations

The best way to use the FAB approach is to think about recognition you have received or the positive things you have done in your past. If, as a producer, you have brought in 10 programs in the last year on time and under budget, then the benefit you can illustrate to your employer is that you know how to work within time and budget restraints. Your accomplishments have demonstrated that, and those money-saving skills will naturally accompany you to the new position.

In another example, your position as manager of a corporate video department for five years may seem like an obvious credit. But you have to turn it into a FAB that your potential employers can understand. If, in those five years, the department increased the number of productions by 50% while expenses remained the same, then that is an accomplishment with a direct benefit to the employer.

The benefit to the potential employer is that you have been successful at cost control and maximization of staff resources. Therefore, your skills can help them. The benefit, then, is that the employer can expect an immediate 10% increase in production from the staff during your first year, and more of the same in succeeding years.

In another example, if, as an editor, four of your programs won awards and those programs received high marks for their editing, then the feature is your experience, the accomplishments are the awards, and the benefits are that you know how to produce award-winning programs and could do that for your new employer.

FAB also works as BAF. You can explain your benefits first to an employer, document them with your accomplishments and end with the features of your background. Look at your resume and determine how your background benefits a new employer. If you are trying to move up the ladder, check how your past successes insure your continued success.

This technique is used by thousands of executive recruiters to get candidates in the door every year to see potential employers. You have to plan your phone calls to contacts to utilize FABs quickly and in an interesting manner. Then, you should be able to set up a meeting.

Percentages are more meaningful than figures. You may be elated with an increase of five productions by your department over the past year. To you it may be a monumental increase- in excess of 40%. But, five productions may be a drop in the bucket to a large teleproduction facility. It is better for you to say, "We had a 42% production increase over last year," rather than state that your department produced five more tapes.

Figures should be used for substantiation, if necessary, but percentages make it simple for employers to relate to.

Go through your background and create FABs to use throughout the entire interview.

CONCLUSION

Looking for a job is a job in itself. It requires you to look at your background and see if it contains the credentials for you to move onward and upward.

If it does not, or if you are just beginning, there are ways to gain the experience you need.

Looking for FABs in your work history enables you to develop the habit of showing employers the benefit of hiring you over someone else. Entering nonbroadcast video and moving up within it requires hard work, but if you are willing to go the extra mile, you will realize your dreams. And that is worth it.

5
Preparing for an Interview

Remember how it felt the first time you went for a job interview?

It might have been the first interview you went on in video, fresh from learning all that good stuff in school, ready to set the world on fire with your ideas, feelings, thoughts and creativity. Perhaps your first interview took place when you needed a summer job to help pay your tuition. Or, maybe, way back when you needed an after-school job to support your record habit.

Remember how you felt? You may have felt a bit anxious, a bit afraid. But you were there because you were interested in getting a job. More than likely, you were there because you were interested in doing what was best for *you,* not necessarily for the betterment of XYZ Cable TV or Amalgamated Industries' video department.

Most people are shocked when they realize that the employer does not share this concern. If the employer is to be successful, he has to be interested primarily in himself, not you, the interviewee. The employer can afford to be self-centered, to look at you and consider what is best for the company. Often, he will take this posture during the interview.

Many times after an interview, I have heard friends and associates say, "I couldn't believe it. I'm the best thing that happened to them and they couldn't see it. I've got the background for this job. I'm trained for it. I could do it with one hand tied behind me. And it'd be great!!! If I could just get that job . . . I'd be doing exactly what I've always wanted to do. How come they can't see that I'm perfect for the job?"

And that is the reason they do not get the job. They are thinking only of what is best for themselves. They never considered what is best for the employer, nor did they take the time and effort to sell themselves to the employer.

THREE BASIC "TRUTHS" OF THE INTERVIEW

There are three basic premises that you should keep in mind in order to build a successful interview strategy: hiring is an important decision for a manager, you cannot afford to appear self-centered during the interview, and you must sell yourself.

Hiring Is an Important Decision

The most important decision many managers make is the hiring decision. It is a decision that reflects strongly on the person who makes it. Success in hiring or an error in judgment can have long-term effects on a manager's career.

If Mr. Jones, the manager, picks the right person for the job, that decision and that person make him look good to his superiors and peers. Often when we hear about people who have been an asset to an organization, we remember who hired that person. Whether Mr. Jones is still with the company or not, he is still given credit for bringing the "find" into the organizational fold.

People usually hire in their own image. A tough, go-getter type of sales manager often feels good surrounded by other high-powered salespeople. Likewise, engineering directors, who are detail-oriented, like to hire those similarly inclined. Because of that, the entire thrust of an organization is built from the ground up with people hired in the image of the managers who do the hiring. If, however, Mr. Jones makes a "bad" choice, the stigma of that poor decision may linger forever and hamper his career.

Even in education, the hiring decision looms large and powerful. A media department director at a large college had a staff (mostly inherited) of over 30 people from different departments, such as art, video, film and graphics, reporting to him. When it came time for the director to hire new department heads, two of the three turned out to be "clunkers." To compound the problem, the director neglected the situation until his superiors eventually had to do the firing. Ultimately the responsibility for hiring new personnel was delegated elsewhere.

In corporations, eyebrows are often raised when turnover in a department exceeds what is considered normal. A high turnover rate often means the manager cannot hire adequately. At the very least, this will stunt his career.

You Cannot Afford to Appear Self-Centered During the Interview

The basic nature of an interview puts Mr. Jones and you at odds with each other from the start. Both of you are interested in your own welfare. You want to do what is right for you in order to get the best position you can. And Mr. Jones wants to hire the best possible candidate for the job. If he does he will look good, and his career will be enhanced.

Because of this, he can afford to be self-centered during the interview. You cannot. He can afford to judge you by whatever criteria he wants. Search and placement firms have concluded that, assuming two candidates' backgrounds and achievements are identical, the employer will *always* hire the one he likes, can relate to and gets along with best.

In other words, if you are going to get the job, then you have to be prepared to get the employer to communicate with you and *like* you. You cannot wait for him to "discover" how good you will be. You have to point out your credentials in such a way that the employer can relate to them and see how well you will work out.

Many qualified candidates cannot communicate with the person across the desk and, therefore, never get the job they want or deserve. This brings us to the third and most important aspect of interviewing strategy.

Learn to Sell Yourself

You must become the advocate or salesperson of the most precious asset any of us have—YOURSELF!

You must show the employer how your experience, background, education, training and attitude will benefit him. The fact that this job opportunity will benefit you is best left to internal discussion with yourself. Remember, the employer does not have to care if you think the job is the greatest thing to happen since night baseball. He only cares what you can do to benefit the business.

Some people think that sales is a less than honorable profession, and that anything that has to be sold to someone must not be very good. After all, if the item or service to be sold is so good (goes this illogical thinking), surely anyone can clearly see its superiority. This kind of thinking will not help you win job offers. Employers need to be sold on you, just as they would on a new tape format or production switcher.

For example, a well-educated man worked for me for a number of years. He had a lot going for him. Not only was his AV/ITV training superior, he had a great deal of practical application experience and a tremendous motivation to do the job quickly and efficiently.

Because he eventually outgrew the job, he started looking for a new one. I gladly helped and gave him several referrals. Although he was well-qualified for most of the jobs, he failed to get past the first interview. This was surprising to me, for he lived and breathed video production and engineering. He knew all the nuances of equipment and could coax a dead piece back to life. He was, in effect, a very thorough nonbroadcast video professional.

Finally, a friend of mine who interviewed him explained the problem. He said, "He dresses poorly, and, even more important, he acts like he's doing *me* a favor by interviewing him!"

Suddenly, it all made sense. He was *qualified*, he had all the right credentials, but he failed miserably in one area. He failed to communicate what he could do for the employer—he failed to sell himself. He felt that he was so good, he did not have to prove it. He thought employers could simply see how great he was.

Employers tend to hire people they like and can relate to. They hire people who will fit in with their present staff and their company. They hire those who will make a significant contribution and will reflect well upon themselves.

Therefore, it is up to you to show them that you are the best person for the job, that you can do it and that you want to do it. (Let us not quibble here that ultimately you may not want the job. For if there is no offer, there is no job to turn down.)

LEARN ABOUT THE COMPANY AND THE JOB

One time, I was explaining a job opening to an exceptionally bright college graduate. Her enthusiasm bubbled. She eagerly wrote down the job requirements and told me she would let me know what happened after she called about it. Suddenly, it happened.

I had mentioned the name of a well-known smokestack industry throughout the conversation. I knew the company, what it made, where the plants were located and the company's function and standing in the local economy. Imagine my surprise when, after I asked her if she knew where the main offices were located she said, "Uh . . . I don't even know how to spell their name!"

The young job aspirant, ready to set up an interview appointment and plunge headlong into an interview, did not know anything about the company. She was in danger of committing a classic cart-before-the-horse mistake.

You must find out all you can about the person and the organization you are talking to before you walk in the door for your meeting. The more you know, the more likely you are to receive an offer. There are many places to look for this information.

One place to get this information could be the company's public relations department. Many publicly held companies have a PR person whose job is to answer questions for the public.

Information on the company is just part of the information you need to prepare for the interview. You need to find out about the employer and the job as well. This preparation will set you apart and can help you ascertain your potential job satisfaction.

Use the Library

The business section of most major public libraries is stocked with in-depth reference guides on virtually all companies and organizations. *Standard and Poor's, Moody's,* and *Dun and Bradstreet* are just a few of the major annual directories that are virtual storehouses of information you can use to learn about the business you are interested in. State and local directories can supply you with additional information. These directories use the Standard Industrial Code (SIC), which is a universal numbering system that groups industries. By using the SIC, you will be able to check out the company's competitors as well.

Annual reports on publicly held companies are easy to obtain. Business sections of most libraries carry hard copy or microfiche copies for several past years. By looking at several years of annual reports you will be able to identify any major changes in personnel or product and service makeup of the company. You will also get an idea of what plans were made and if management succeeded at implementing them.

From this information, you can put together a comprehensive analysis of the organization you are dealing with. Often, reading what is between the lines is as important as what is published.

For example, some questions you should ask yourself include: What are the company's specific products and services? Have they changed? What is its market, its sales volume, both past and present? Has the company grown or shrunk? Why? What are the reasons they give for the direction in which they are moving? And what do you think the reasons are?

Contact Professional Organizations

Not only are professional organizations good places to network for finding a job, they are exceptionally good for finding out nitty-gritty details about the position and the person you will be interviewing with.

Things you will want to know include: who you will work with, the working environment, who the boss is and what he/she is like, what the organizational culture is like, what is expected of you, what are the duties and responsibilities of the job (producer can mean many different things) as well as what extras are required (travel, late night meetings, weekend hours), and what happened to the last person who held the position.

This information prepares you for the interview. Your knowledge about the position, people, boss and company will spark the employer's interest in you.

Organizations like ITVA, the Association of Multi-Image (AMI), Public Relations Society of America (PRSA) and International Association of Business Communications (IABC) have meetings and membership directories that you can use. (See Appendix C at the back of this book for addresses.) Contact people who might know the person you are interviewing with or at least lhe organization you are talking to and find out what they know. Employment counselors will tell you that "chemistry makes the hire." You must create the chemistry.

If the job you interview for is to replace someone, it is as important to find out if the person was promoted as it is to find out why the employee was let go. A promotion gives you an idea of the career path others have taken before you and what you might be able to expect. Conversely, a firing may let you know what is or is not acceptable in the position and will tell you something about the organization.

Learn About the Industry

If you are looking at a position in corporate television, concentrate on understanding what the company does. Think about the company's markets and related industries. Learn about the industry the company is in. Is it the largest or the smallest in the industry? What does its product (or service) do?

Who does the company sell to? This line of thought is very important in determining how the business might react to recessions and booms. For example, building materials and automotive industries often are highly cyclical; good times are usually great, but bad times could mean the loss of your job. This is particularly true when the company follows the axiom: last hired, first fired.

Try to discover how the corporate television department fits in with the goals and objectives of the company. Is the department responsible for training, marketing, internal or external public relations, advertising or customer services?

How large is the facility? What kind and types of equipment do they have? One source for this information is the *Video Register and Teleconferencing Resources Directory* (published by Knowledge Industry Publications, Inc., White Plains, NY). It might be to your advantage to have worked with the same equipment before.

Who does the department report to? This can tell you a lot. Reporting to the director of training means something entirely different from reporting to the vice president of public relations. Furthermore, it will tell you what skills and background you should emphasize in the interview. For example, reporting to the training department requires you to talk about and prove your credentials in instructional media. Conversely, reporting to public relations demands that you explain your successes in image-building as well as your background in dealing with the media.

If possible, you should know the names of corporate officers and where the factories or stores are located. You want to become as expert on the industry as possible. The more you show that you know about them, the more enthusiastic they will be about hiring you.

A case in point: I once had an interview with a large multinational corporation. The position was to start up and build a corporate video department. It was an exciting opportunity and I left nothing to chance. In the weeks preceding my appointment, I poured over every annual report, every newspaper article and every piece of information I could find about the company.

I copied all the information into handwritten notes. I studied them and tried to internalize as much information about the company as I could. It meant a lot to me; I really wanted the job.

After an exhausting morning of interviews, I had lunch with the person who would be my supervisor. Over coffee he said, ". . . Well, Bronson doesn't feel that we should be going in that direction."

Not missing a beat, I added, "Well, coming from engineering, as he does, the conservative approach is probably what he's most comfortable with."

What happened here is that we had exchanged conversation about the CEO and I had made the point, subtly but effectively, that I had gone to the trouble of doing my homework. I would later find out that the seemingly innocuous lunch conversation played a major part in the company extending me the offer.

In another instance, a lucrative video department directorship was available in a large midwestern transportation firm. The former incumbent had resigned to head a larger division in a larger company in an area of the country he wanted to move to.

Seven very qualified candidates from a variety of industries and production houses made it to the final interview. They all demonstrated their capabilities. But the majority of them (and I suspect all of them) were guilty of not doing their homework on the company. For, when it came time to choose a replacement, the person picked was not one of the seven, but someone with a less extensive video background from a smaller transportation company. Clearly, the employer valued someone who understood and could relate to the industry, not just nonbroadcast video.

If You Are Interviewing for a Job in Cable

In cable, it's important to understand who the company is and what its services are. At the local level, you should know what its programming is and if it is a division of a larger company. *Broadcasting/Cablecasting Yearbook* and *Cable Contacts* both give inside information on individual cable operators (e.g., department heads, markets served, services, number of employees).[1]

You should be familiar with the kind of programming the company provides and what it produces. Try to view some programming. If you have to, have a friend record several hours of programming for you to watch. You should also know which communities the cable company serves since each CATV station has an obligation to provide public access.

If You Are Interviewing for a Production House Job

Production houses vary widely in size and scope. Find out what clients the production house serves and what services it offers. A quick look at the company's rate card will tell you many of the answers. Try to get a copy of the rate card *before* your interview. Local professional contacts and even competitors might have valuable information for you.

If the rate card shows prices for 1-inch post-production, you should be prepared to talk about the success *you* have had in 1-inch post-production. If multi-image prices are listed, your experience with programming multi-slide projector shows is what you will discuss. It is possible that this particular experience could be the edge you need to get the job.

---

[1] *Broadcasting/Cablecasting Yearbook* (Broadcasting Publications, Inc., 1735 De Sales Street N.W., Washington, DC 20036) and *Cable Contacts Yearbook* (Larimi Communications Associates, Ltd., 151 East 50th Street, New York, NY 10022).

DRESS FOR SUCCESS

Michael was ready for the job interview. His resume was nicely typed, his resume reel was edited and he even planned to be early to the appointment.

"So," I said, shaking his hand, "you're leaving, going home first?"

"Nah," he replied. "I'm just going to kill a few hours and then get there about 15 minutes early."

I was confused. I was afraid to ask, but I did anyway. "Wait a minute. What are you wearing to the interview?"

"Why this, of course." He gestured to his blue jeans and corduroy jacket, plaid shirt and blue tie. He was wearing some kind of brown boots as well. "Anything wrong?"

"Plenty," I said. Because, I explained, if he intended to go to the interview dressed as he was, he had little chance of getting the job. His casual attire would interfere with the employer's more formal expectations.

Several nonbroadcast video production-types have informed me that they regard what they wear to be an extension of their creative style. The logic seems to be: this is really me so take me as I am because creative people dress weird and everyone knows it.

Fine. This may be true. But do not expect to get much in the way of a lucrative job in the industry. Nonbroadcast television is tied too tightly to business organizations to extend creative license to the dress code.

I have seen Hollywood producer Francis Ford Coppola in his open shirt and full beard. I know Jim Henson, creator of the Muppets, always shows up looking like a 1960s hippie. And I have seen Eddie Murphy in his leather suits. They all look very casual and comfortable and I am sure that their clothes are a reflection of what they are truly like.

But they are not going to a job interview with Eagleton University or United Monstrosity Industries. You are. And the people who interview you are going to be judging *you*. First impressions are made within the first five minutes of meeting someone. And that means employers have barely shaken your hand, sat you down, made small conversation, and asked maybe one pertinent question before deciding whether or not to hire you.

Obviously, you have little time to make a favorable impression. Therefore, anything you can do to help that impression will improve your chances.

You may object, "But I will be wearing casual clothes 90% of the time when I'm acting in my capacity as a production assistant." And you're right, some nonbroadcast organizations have an unwritten policy regarding dress based on the types of jobs being done. When you tour the facility, you may see others dressed more casually than you are. But remember, one of the basic tenets of the interview is that you have to sell yourself to the employer. And a conservatively dressed salesperson with a professional manner has a better chance of obtaining the job.

Appropriate Interview Attire

To help you dress for success, the employment industry in general recommends several rules for interviews.

John Malloy, in his book *Dress for Success*, explains that conservative business suits, ties, shirts or blouses and shined leather shoes should be worn to job interviews.[2]

Try to find out how people dress for their jobs. It is the general rule to dress two levels above the job you are interviewing for. If employees in the position wear white shirts and blouses without coats, then a suit would be appropriate for your meeting.

Generally, navy suits are appropriate for men and women. White shirts are always a good choice. In fact, I know of companies where they are the unwritten rule. A tasteful red tie completes the ensemble.

Women should appear feminine, but not sexy. Some makeup is fine, but obvious eyeliner and blush and heavy perfume are out.

---

[2] John Malloy, *Dress for Success* (New York, Warner Books, 1976).

Midsize heels or flats are good; high heels are not. As with men, navy suits with a small tie are preferable and, of course, a white blouse. Jewelry should not be flashy and kept to a minimum. Earrings must be conservative.

Many of us in the nonbroadcast television business, who must carry equipment and still attend executive meetings, keep different sets of clothes in our offices. I have come down off the lighting grid in jeans and tennis shoes only to stop in my office and change back into my suit in order to answer the CEO's call. If you think that is ludicrous, just make one trip down "mahogany row" in your jeans, hear the reactions and you will never do it again.

In certain parts of the country, regional wear is accepted in the business community. In those instances, you may bend toward the trend. Cowboy boots, for instance, are always acceptable in Texas. To stay on the safe side, though, the conservative business look will always serve you well.

One of the questions I like applicants to ask is what they should wear on the job. The reason I like it is that it allows most employers to explain the company's human side and gives candidates information about the culture of the organization. It is information that can help everyone determine if the chemistry is right. Some organizations demand three-piece suits. Others emphasize sport-coat fashions and some flair; and a few use the sweater and jeans look.

When in doubt, be conservative. No one has been refused a job offer because he or she dressed too well. But many times the opposite is true.

BODY LANGUAGE

Hold your head up throughout all the interviews you attend. It helps you to look confident. When you meet someone, look him or her straight in the eye. Looking down makes you appear meek. Looking away makes you appear shifty and untrustworthy.

When people shake your hand, make it a firm handshake. People get a lot out of that contact. Of course, do not let it be a bone crusher either.

Think about some of the people you know. The people you tend to admire have good posture and a striking stature. No one wants to hire someone who appears tired and listless with rounded shoulders and a sagging gut.

What you say via body language is very important, especially in the interview's critical opening moments.

CONCLUSION

The first five minutes of a job interview are the most important. How you look, act and what you say are critical because that is when most people make up their minds about you as a person.

Do not be self-centered during the interview. Try to sell yourself to the employer. Resumes, resume reels and qualifications briefs (discussed in Chapter 7) can further your cause once you have made that initial first good impression. How you look and behave at the interview are almost as important as what you say. The hiring decision is very important for employers. By doing your homework on the organization, you can conduct yourself intelligently and with confidence. People hire people, not paper. Preparation can make you a winner in your job search.

6
Handling Interview Questions

In this chapter we will discuss how to answer many of the questions that will come up during your interviews. We will explain how to respond to them and will cover the types of questions you should be prepared to ask.

Imagine this. The interview has gone well. You have radiated poise, intelligence, warmth. You care about the company, school, or facility and you have shown it. You've done your homework on the company, and it has paid off. You really like the employer, and he/she really likes you. You are pretty certain you have the inside track on this job.

You have answered all the questions about your personality, about yourself, about your motives, about the salary, about your background—just like you rehearsed—perfectly! In fact, you can't think of anything that is going to prevent you from getting the job. You are just about to ask when the dental and health plans will kick in. When suddenly . . . you feel the roof is starting to cave in . . . suddenly the air is very warm . . . in fact, it feels downright hot. You would like some air, but you can't breathe . . . you feel a tightening in your chest. The employer you were interviewing with is no longer that nice, friendly guy . . . in fact, he has turned into the Grand Inquisitor! What is happening? You can't even speak. Why?

WELCOME TO THE LAND OF TOUGH QUESTIONS

Tough questions are the ones you would rather not discuss. The ones you wish they would not ask. But they always do and they always will. So, learn to deal with them.

105

What is a tough question? A tough question is any question you would rather not answer, such as:

- Why did you leave a particular job?
- Why were you fired?
- Why are you willing to accept a job that pays less than your current one?
- Why did your salary decrease at some time in your past?
- Why have you had several jobs over the past few years?
- Why have personality problems arisen in past positions?
- Why were you unemployed for a long period of time?

These questions should not surprise you. In fact, you should take a long hard look at your past experiences, locate problem areas and be prepared to explain them— at length, if necessary—at any interview.

Why Did You Leave Your Last Position?

There are many good reasons for leaving a job. Sometimes they are not evident to those who are not familiar with your situation. Mass layoffs, corporate takeovers or elimination of divisions and departments are not that rare today.

Employers are becoming increasingly aware that wholesale firings and layoffs are an integral part of corporate America. If this is why you left your job, by all means, tell the interviewer.

As takeovers and mergers continue, good, quality people with usable skills are frequently caught in the middle and lose their jobs. It could happen to you. If it has happened, do not assume it is negative. Chances are your potential employer will not view it as negative either.

Or maybe your last job was not what you thought it would be. Perhaps the parameters of the job were changed due to circumstances beyond your control. Perhaps the company or division you were working for went in a direction you did not want to go.

You may have left your last position because the job was tedious and you are capable of doing more. In this case, you will increase your stock with the employer by simply telling the truth.

Or, you may have liked the job and everything about it, but, due to budgetary restraints or departmental rules, you could not afford to continue at the available salary. Educational ITV departments and local CATV stations often have this problem holding on to good people.

Remember, you *have* to have a good reason. It may be that you took time off to "get your head together and now you know what you want," but a good reason has to be arrived at by you in terms of the employer's needs. Employers, after all, are human too! They probably sowed a few wild oats when they were young.

If any of these scenarios hold true for you, by all means, say so. Be prepared to back up your statements with any evidence you can assemble. Remember, the employer you are talking to is thinking of his welfare first. He needs to uncover any potential problem areas before you start to work for his company. That is why tough questions are asked.

Do not be defensive. Understand that the questions will be asked, and that you should prepare, ahead of time, to answer them completely. Practice your answers with a friend or spouse in a simulated interview session.

What Were You Doing in Tibet for Two Years?

You were in Tibet in order to better yourself. You wanted to grow. You needed time for yourself. You needed to get that out of your system. But now you know what you want to do and this job is it.

A long period of unemployment, particularly in the fast changing world of video, will be questioned. Again, do not act defensively. Expect the question and be prepared.

It is entirely possible that you rejected several job offers during the unemployment period while waiting for the right opportunity. Let the interviewer know if you had freelance jobs, or attended educational courses, seminars or workshops during this period. These kinds of activities will show that you have kept in touch with the industry.

It is no longer taboo to take a few years off from your career. While it will not advance your career or allow you to keep compensational pace with your contemporaries, it has become acceptable to take time to study one's options. Many employers, in fact, appreciate such candor from a candidate.

If you needed time to assess your career while trying some other things, then say so. But make it crystal clear that that time of reflection or of trying other career options made you absolutely certain that this is the industry you want to be in and that this is the job you want. No wavering, no meditation. That is it. The employer is human. We all like to be around people who like what they do and know where they are going.

Questionable Questions

Pregnancy and raising a family is seen as an acceptable reason for women to leave the work force. For those liberated men who took time off to raise little Rodney and Sue, however, it is a tough sell. Childcare arrangements, however, are expected to change dramatically in the next decade because, by 1992, women will make up over 50% of the work force.

In 1964, the federal government enacted a law that forbids discrimination in employment based upon race, color, religion, sex, national origin and age. There are often related city and state codes that prohibit discrimination in hiring based on marital status and physical handicaps as well.[1] The broader of any overlapping statutes are the ones employers must adhere to. Questions that

---

[1] Bernard Frechtman, *Employment Agency Law* (New York: Association of Personnel Consultants of New York State, 1981), pp. 36–47.

categorize applicants in these areas should not be asked during an interview.

A question in an employment interview cannot be asked of a man if it cannot be asked of a woman. Employers cannot ask a woman if she is married, if she is pregnant, if she is planning a pregnancy, or what she will do if she becomes pregnant. Likewise, interviewers are prohibited from asking a man if he's married, contemplating having children, or intends to take time off for birthing or raising the kids.

Questions about who takes care of the kids during the day and what happens to them when the school year ends cannot be asked. Essentially, the laws were enacted to eliminate bigotry in the hiring process.

Naturally, unscrupulous employers may ask you these questions in spite of the law. And they may deny you employment based on these illegal questions. If you feel you have been discriminated against, charges can be filed with the local office of the Equal Employment Opportunity Commission. Practically speaking, however, without documented proof, such cases are very difficult to prove. Even with proof, filing a claim is time-consuming and can prevent you from pursuing other offers. You may be totally within your rights, but it is in the best interests of most organizations to avoid legal problems.

On the other hand, the federal government now requires you to prove citizenry status for every job you take, so be prepared to show your birth certificate, naturalization papers or work card. Failure to do so can prevent you from getting a job.

Employers are permitted to ask you about any relatives who work for the company, particularly if the company has anti-nepotism rules. Courts have upheld such rules even when the familial connection is distant.

It Says Here, You Were Fired

According to Robert Half, a leading authority on employment, 70% of all people have, at one time or another, been fired.

If this has happened to you, you are not alone, and losing a job does not necessarily mean that you are a failure. If it helps you during the interview, you should think about the fact that there is a good chance that the employer sitting across from you, too, has probably been fired at some time.

My personal termination story is not very elegant. I was living in Denver, CO, newly married, and struggling to pay the rent. But I was enjoying my new career as a radio advertisement time salesman. My station had a new country music format that I hated, but I was determined to succeed.

I had been there for only three months. I worked hard to learn what an Arbitron was, how to read it, how it could be sold for or against, where the advertising agencies were, how they bought time, what accounts were available and how I could sell my station's time to them.

It did not help that I was not at all familiar with Denver. (I quickly learned, however, that everyone in Denver was from someplace else.) I was lost most of the time. And my shoot-from-the-hip style of salesmanship did not win me many friends in the agencies. But I was hungry, aggressive, and, most important to me, I was in the media. I had finally made it. Four years of college plus a master's degree were finally paying off.

I was very excited. So excited that when the sales manager asked to see me, the second highest billing salesman, along with the highest billing salesman, I actually thought he was going to thank us for a job well done.

Instead, we were fired. The sales manager was against it, but the general manager had given the order. And neither of us ever knew why.

I thought I was out of the media for good. After all, who would hire someone who had just been fired from his very first job in the industry.

I felt that a large red "F" for fired was attached to my chest, and any employer ever interviewing me again would see the letter, smell a loser and throw me out of his office. I was positive that I would have to spend the rest of my life selling pencils or washing windows, rather than doing what I had always wanted to do.

Barely one week later, a sales manager I had interviewed with months earlier learned that I had been unceremoniously fired and telephoned me.

"I heard you got popped," he said. My spirits dropped. Did this mean it was all over the tight little advertising community?

"Yeah, me and Denny. I just don't know why . . . ." My voice trailed off.

"So, why don't you come and see me?" he prodded. So I did. I explained what had happened to the best of my knowledge and added that my former sales manager had promised to give me a good recommendation in spite of the general manager's actions. I assume he checked it out because he called the next day. Once again, I was selling radio time. And I have been "in the media biz" ever since.

The point of my story is that getting canned is not necessarily the end of the world. You will still be able to get another job in the field if you handle the problem of a termination with suitable candor and preparation.

When handling the tough questions about a termination, prepare your answers in advance. You should be honest with yourself and others, and do a little homework.

Often, a former employer, if asked, will work with you on explaining a termination problem. People have become sophisticated about this. Not everyone works out perfectly in every situation. Problems do occur.

If the reasons for the termination were yours and yours only, admit your shortcomings and explain how you have learned from your mistakes. Statements, such as "I've matured since that time to realize . . ." or "Now that I've been in a position of supervision, I can appreciate the other side and have learned from my mistakes." can turn a negative into an actual positive.

Sometimes, the help of a former immediate supervisor cannot be enlisted.

For example, a writer I have known for years had a tremendous video background in the medical area. With several awards to her credit and the abilities to act as a director, producer, writer and interviewer, as well as her flexibility in working with a number of different people, she was well-known and respected.

But a new boss moved in above her, and soon the sparks began to fly. It became apparent that one or the other would have to leave, and the new boss certainly was not about to.

In this case the new boss would not help. But, by discreetly contacting her former boss, a good recommendation from someone who knew her prior work history could be obtained.

When your immediate supervisor cannot be used as a reference, you should secure the services of someone within your old organization who knew exactly what you did and can talk sensibly about it.

THE FOUR MAIN INTERVIEW QUESTIONS

An interview is basically a fact-finding mission. The interviewer asks you certain questions and your answers determine whether you will get the job. While all interviews are different, there are four basic types of questions the employer may ask you: the "tell me about yourself" question, personality questions, motivation questions and salary expectation questions. The best way to answer them is to follow the basic question–answering rule: **Always answer questions in terms of your background and qualifications. If that is not possible, answer them in terms of the job's requirements.**

The "Tell Me About Yourself" Question

Interviewees are often puzzled by this question. They either think that it is frivolous and does not have to be answered, or that the employer wants to hear every little detail that the interviewee can remember. Neither interpretation, of course, is true.

The "tell me about yourself" question is asked to find out some of your qualifications for the position. Employers do not want to know every detail about your life, nor do they want to hear "Uh, well there isn't really much to tell." This *is* the interview and the interviewer is giving you a golden opportunity to take the offensive.

When an employer asks you to tell about yourself, assume he or she is asking you to tell about your qualifications for the position. Start with your educational background and how it qualifies you. Explain your work history and how those experiences qualify you. Be prepared to describe each job, from the past to the present in terms of a single indication of accomplishment. It is important that you explain your accomplishments and benefits. If you do, the employer will then be able to see how your background will directly benefit the company.

If you ramble while answering this question, the employer may sense indecision on your part. If you try to say the things you think he or she wants to hear, your mannerisms will betray you and show your lack of confidence.

There is no one right way to answer this question. But I have heard some examples that follow the rule and make the point.

A Producer Seeking a Producer Position in a Larger Company

I started in film at Ithaca College. I always wanted to make movies. After completing my B.S., I stayed in upstate New York working on different films.

I moved back home two years later after I figured there was little chance of my making enough money to survive. I did some odd jobs while looking for a position, and one of the jobs I interviewed for was an AV technician job. They told me I was overqualified, but would keep my resume on file. I expected nothing to come of it, but three weeks later they called me back to interview for another job opening in their nonbroadcast area. I was there for 12 years and moved from a production assistant to department head. Training, point-of-purchase, news programs—I produced them all. Usually, I wrote the program, selected the talent, shot it, edited it and obtained the client's approval—an approval that almost always came. I rarely had to reedit something.

I love the freedom of working in nonbroadcast. The proof of the quality of my work is my resume reel, my scripts and the number of clients who liked the productions that I did for them. Also, I received about 20 awards for my shows.

I enjoy nonbroadcast. There's freedom in the creative process and I'm good at it. I love to produce and would like to do it for you.

An Editor/Director Seeking a Department Head Job

When I was in college I worked in catering. After six months I was promoted to the supervisor of the candy store with two assistants.

I always knew I wanted to be in television, so I took a position selling consumer TVs, VCRs and cameras. Although I was good at it, I knew I wanted to get into television production.

I had heard about a series of AV and video courses at the local junior college, so I inquired and took the television production courses. During summer break I volunteered to help teach the production classes. It was there that I did my first editing. In a short time I was hooked. I loved to create programs, and editing is, for me, the real core of creativity.

While working at the video store, a customer heard about my production interests and told me that the company where he worked had purchased some video equipment and needed help running it. He gave me the phone number of the training director, and I called.

They hired me, and in five years our little department made over 60 different programs. The department grew, and so did my responsibilities. I now have two full-time people under me and am responsible for hiring all the freelancers who augment our staff for the different shows. We now produce about 40 programs a year, and

I'm responsible for all of them. I work on schedules, budgeting, talent selection, and direct most of the production and all of the post-production. I work with our CEO on down to the secretaries. Our department has been very successful, and I have been a major contributor to that, evidenced by the change in my responsibilities from production to supervision.

I know I can run a nonbroadcast department efficiently and effectively—because that's what I've been doing for the past three years. And any time I find that I need additional skills, I go and get them.

An Entry-Level Production Assistant Looking For That First Job

I have always been interested in television, particularly nonbroadcast television. I feel that I can be more creative in nonbroadcast because I can do more and learn more. I am very organized and like to do a variety of different things. And I want to be the best at what I do.

I know my background isn't as extensive as I'd like, but with this position I know I could contribute immediately and work on any production in any capacity you'd choose. I've got some editing experience on CMX and VideoMedia and I've shot with Ikegami, Sony and Hitachi cameras.

Because of my production internship with the Institute for Higher Education I know my way around a studio and feel comfortable on remote shoots. Two summers ago I was a photographer's assistant and learned the art of shot composition. I think that's helped prepare me for shooting and editing. People tell me I have a good "eye."

I've tried to keep my production experience as broad as possible so that I could be helpful in a number of different areas. From what you've told me, I know I could help you here.

Professor/Department Head Seeking Producer/Director
Position in a Corporate Setting

I remember one answer I gave to the "tell me about yourself" question. I said, in part:

> I have always been able to take situations where nothing existed and make something out of it. I enjoy doing that. When I started at Metro TV, we started in a shell of an office—the drywall hadn't even been put in place. But I dug in and started building instructional training tapes for one, two and then eventually a number of departments. Within a year we had established ourselves as the premier educational media tool and had people coming to us to develop instructional programs.
>
> In a way, I've been in training all my life. As a professor, I had to train students to operate television equipment. Several of my students went on to new careers in the television industry. As director of instructional video, I learned how to take concepts and translate them to video for maximum training effectiveness. Ten different programs in our five years of existence won awards for excellence in achievement. What we set as goals, we reached.
>
> As I said, I like to take nothing and make it into something special. And I know I can do it for you.

Yes, I was hired.

Hint

Prepare a five- to ten-minute presentation describing your accomplishments before you interview. This way, you will feel confident as you speak. You'll realize that you have gained an advantage over less well prepared candidates by preparing ahead of time.

The "tell me about yourself" question allows one of the few opportunities for you to take the offensive during the interview. Until that point, the interviewer is asking you questions and directing the conversation. By preparing ahead of time, you can take the spotlight and shine it where you think you will look the best for the job. It is important to seize this moment.

The Personality Questions

Employers ask personality questions to determine whether you are the kind of person they want to hire. You can recognize these questions during the interview because the answer is usually obvious.

Recently a man in his forties, with a wife and two children to support, discussed a career change with me. He wanted to leave education and move into corporate video.

I suggested he contact a production house that recently had a change "at the top." Via a phone call, he found that they were interested in him and he set up an interview with the president of the firm.

Two weeks later, he stopped by looking for other referrals. When I asked him what had happened at the production house he recounted the interview. "You know," he said, "he asked me if I worked well under pressure or deadlines."

"Great," I said, anticipating his obvious answer to a personality question.

"Great, nothing," he scowled. "I told him that if they expect true creativity from this guy [pointing to himself], I need the time to do the job right. I'm not about to move into a place where they are going to expect me to move mountains in seconds."

"But," I sputtered, "That wasn't the point of the question, he just wanted to know . . . ."

"Then he asked if I was creative." He continued. "And I told him that I was as creative as the next guy is . . . ."

And on and on it went. The employer asked a question with an obvious answer. And he rebutted each one as if he were in a debate.

Some people seem to have a rule about using the obvious answer. They seem to think that if the answer is obvious, it must be some kind of trick question. Even if they feel positive about the question, they feel they should argue it.

When you are asked a personality question with an obvious answer do not claim perfection. Do answer it honestly. If possible, provide an example from your past to substantiate your response.

For example:

Question: Are you creative?
Answer: Yes. On my last job, I directed [wrote, produced, etc.] a program that received three different awards for production excellence.

Question: Do you get along well with people?
Answer: Yes. In my last position, I worked successfully with vice presidents, marketing directors, even our advertising agency. I know I can get my point across to them, but I still hear their wants and needs and can work with them to make the project go.

Question: Can you work under pressure or deadlines?
Answer: Of course. In my department, if you didn't get the job to the client on time, you weren't there the next day. I was there for eight years, and had several people comment how they couldn't believe I made the deadline, but I did. I've worked late or on weekends to get a job done on time.

Question: Why do you think you can do this job?
Answer: Because I have done it in the past. And I've done it well! For example, last year I not only crewed 40 different programs, but I produced five of them as well.

Question: Can you take a script, rewrite it if it needs it, work
              with the client, shoot it, edit it, have it approved and
              out the door in less than a week?

Answer: [Remember: Don't claim perfection.] Well, I'd have
              to see the specific project first, but just last month
              for Patton Junior College, I took a 20-page script
              and . . . .

Question: Tell me . . . are you a success?

Answer: Yes, I think I am. For the last three years, I was given
              a raise higher than anyone else in the division based
              on my . . . . [you can answer this affirmatively by
              describing promotions, salary increases, awards and
              any other notable achievements you have received
              that point out that you are, indeed, a success].

Hint

Plan on handling personality questions with the obvious
answer and a short example from your history that illustrates the
truth of your answer.

The Motivation Questions

Motivation questions are asked to determine whether you
would really like doing the job that is available. Employers prefer
to hire people who really want to do the job. If you are selective
in your answers and answer the question well, motivation questions can help you in your job search.

When dealing with motivation questions it is important to
answer clearly and concisely. They are asked to determine the
amount of "fire" you have for the position. Employers ask them
to determine your motivation for the position and to help them
decide whether you would really like to do the available job.

Here are some sample motivation questions and possible answers:

Question: Tell me, what would be the ideal job for you?

Answer: Well, the ideal job for me would be one that . . . [You would answer in terms of the position you are interviewing for.]

Question: Well, you know, International Widget here is a large corporation. But sometimes people are more comfortable with a smaller corporation, you know what I mean, one that's more personal. Would you rather work for a large or small company?

Answer: Oh, I'd rather work for a large company like I.W. I feel that the volume of work would be greater here, and I could make a stronger impact in a shorter time and really contribute to the goals of the department as well as the company.

Question: Let's say that you didn't have to work for a living. Perhaps you won the lottery or inherited a large amount of money. If you didn't have to work for a living, what would you do?

Answer: I'd stay exactly in the same field I'm in now. I love television and I know that I'm really good at what I do in it. I'd just have to keep working in corporate television somewhere. I might buy a newer car or a bigger house, but I'd stay in video.

Question: How much money do you expect to be making five years from now?

Answer: Oh, well in about five years I could see a cost-of-living increase plus a reasonable percentage for good work. I know I'd do well. [This question needs to be answered carefully in terms of the job that is offered. A $20,000 editor's position will not blossom into a $100,000 position in 10 or even 20 years. Think about what cost-of-living raises are like and answer based on those figures.]

Question: What would you say is your biggest weakness?

Answer: My biggest weakness would be [answer with something that's not really a weakness] my tendency to push my people too hard when a deadline is nearing.

Motivation questions are easy to answer. They beg for the answer the employer wants to hear. Simply tell the interviewer that, but never lie or stretch the truth. Prepare your answer before the interview and always answer in terms of the position.

The Salary Question

Generally speaking, it is best not to discuss salary until the position is offered to you. Young, would-be producers with excellent backgrounds go into interviews for jobs that they would give their right arms for, but blow their chances by not handling the salary question properly.

I know this sounds like a broken record, but this is where homework on the position, company and employer really pays off. You should try to determine the salary parameters for the job before you walk in the door for the interview. If this is not possible, the industry surveys listed in Appendix B at the back of this book will give you a good approximation.

Common sense is also a factor in your attempt to figure out what the position pays. The word "assistant" always pays less than a definable job title like "editor" or "writer." An assistant producer makes less than a producer. A production assistant is paid less than a director, editor or videographer.

Conversely, positions that interface with top executives or deal with major projects will be higher up on the pay scale. The department's director probably will have a salary commensurate with other directors within the company.

If you can put the salary question off until you have actually been offered the job, you will be dealing from a position of strength. You will probably receive a more favorable offer if they have already decided to hire you.

But employers often bring the question up early in the interview. Sometimes they are attempting to make sure that both parties are talking about similar compensation so that it does not become a problem later on in the hiring process. Other times, it is an attempt to determine a knockout factor or "red flag."

By making salary a red flag you can almost hear the comments after the interview: "Yeah, she's good, but she wants almost $40,000 to start. Heck, I'm the boss and I don't even make that." Or, "I like him, but there's something wrong. I mean, with his background and experience, he said he'd be willing to start at $15,000. And he's married and has a house! Something's wrong for him to want to live on nothing just to make a move."

If you fill out an application for the position, when you get to the question regarding *salary* or *minimum salary expected*, write in "open" or "negotiable." That way, you will not be locked into any figure. If you answer the salary question too early, you raise the possibility of being knocked out of consideration. And it may be that you would take the compensation the employer intended to offer. Once the employer decides to hire you, he does not want to lose you by making an inadequate offer.

While you are in the interview, your mission is to get through it, sell yourself and not agree to an exact figure. If the employer persists, a good way to handle the salary question is "Over at Quantum Productions, my current salary is $35,000 a year. While I do expect an increase, I really don't know enough about the specific opportunity here to give you an exact figure. Could you tell me, please, what . . . " (Take the offensive now and ask a question.)

If you are currently employed in the industry, you should seek a 10% to 15% increase above your current earnings. Unemployed individuals need to be realistic. The same salary as the last one is considered equitable.

Employers do not live in a vacuum. They know what is going on salary-wise in other organizations throughout the nation. If they want you and you are currently doing the job for someone else, they know they have to make an attractive offer to get you to change.

If they offer you the job and the salary is what you expected, ACCEPT IT!

However, if the offer is below your requirement, it is best not to reject the job immediately. Express interest and ask for a few days to think it over. Sometimes, another person can act as a sounding board to help you decide. The extra time can buy you leverage in your negotiations. But do not take too long. Too much time has been known to kill deals.

Later, if you decide the offer is too low, be candid and explain why you think so. But, keep yourself open to ideas. Often, a package can be developed that is worth more than an increased salary. Moving expenses, a travel allowance, a company car, family health insurance or additional life insurance are benefits that can increase the overall package to an acceptable level. For example, a Fortune 500 firm had a problem closing the hiring of a department head for their video department. An increase in salary was not enough to entice its top pick. But after discussions revealed the candidate's concerns regarding selling his old home and relocating, the company revealed its generous home purchase plan. With that package, the deal was closed, and both parties were satisfied. If salary is an obstacle, look for a creative way to get around the problem.

QUESTIONS YOU SHOULD ASK

When going on a job interview, many candidates think that they are there simply to answer all the employer's questions. Most job applicants never realize that they can put themselves at the head of the list of potential hires by asking the employer some of the questions they would like answered.

Often, candidates seem afraid to ask questions. It is as if they think they will be reprimanded for being curious. Nothing could be further from the truth.

By asking the employer the right questions you will actually be creating a more positive impression that will help you obtain more job offers.

Asking questions about the job is your opportunity to decide if it is the right move for you. It is as important that you feel completely informed about the job as it is for the employer to feel completely informed about you. You are making an important decision that will have great ramifications on your life. It is important to have as much information as you need to make the intelligent choice.

When you ask questions, you are showing employers that you are interested in the job, the company or organization, and the *interviewer*. And all of us like it when people are interested in us. There are five basic rules to remember when asking questions during the interview.

Rules for Asking Questions

Rule 1: Be Prepared

In your research you unearthed a lot of information about the organization. There are probably a number of questions that would help you understand the things you have read and heard. Now, during the interview, would be a perfect time to ask those questions. By asking questions based on your research, you are demonstrating to the employer that you have done your homework and are truly interested in the job and company.

Furthermore, practice asking your questions just like you practice the rest of your interview. This will enable you to phrase them correctly and will serve as a check for you to get answers to the questions that you need.

Rule 2: Be Conversational

This is not an inquisition, so make certain that you ask questions at the appropriate time. And take care not to cross-examine the employer. Be natural and not pushy.

Rule 3: Do Not Interrupt

Let the employer complete his train of thought and thereby answer the question the way he or she wants. By practicing good listening skills you appear interested and you may be able to pick up some of the inferences that tell you a great deal about the company and the position.

Rule 4: Use Good Interviewing Techniques

If you are in video, you know that good interviewing techniques open up the conversation and make it flow. Try to avoid questions that can be answered with a simple yes or no. Use the four Ws and the H of asking questions: Who, What, Where, Why and How.

Rule 5: Always Ask Job-related Questions

Prior to the interview, you should prepare a list of 20 to 30 questions about the position, the employer and the company. Take the list with you and when the appropriate time comes, use the list for cues. Such preparation on your part tends to impress employers.

If you think that making up 20 to 30 questions before the interview is an onerous task, remember that many positions require as much time and effort as your personal life. One-third of your daily life and almost half of your waking hours are spent in job-related activities.

If your position is like many described in this book, then you are spending more than 40 hours per week on the job. Television is an intensive business, and the combination of business and television often requires extra effort.

Types of Questions You Should Ask

There are five basic areas that you should cover with your questions.

Interest Questions

Interest questions show that you are interested in the position. Basically, all questions relevant to the position are interest questions.

During the interview, do not wait for the employer to ask if you have any questions. Rather, ask questions while you and the employer are discussing the position and the company.

Do not forget to ask about the employer. Everyone likes to talk about himself or herself, and the employer is no exception.

People-oriented questions are the best type to start your questioning with. Ask about who your peers will be on the job. Ask about possible future subordinates and superiors. Ask what their duties are, what the employer perceives as their strengths and how your position fits in.

Possible interest questions are:

"How did you get to your present position?"
"Who writes the productions?"
"How does the director's position work with mine?"
"Where do the scripts go after they are approved?"
"How does the production assistant's position relate to mine?"

Job Satisfaction Questions

Job satisfaction questions deal with the importance of the position and the factors that motivate employees. By asking them, you indirectly tell the employer your goals and ambitions. By asking several job satisfaction questions, the employer may conclude that you are a highly motivated individual. You should concentrate on the authority given to you to carry out the job, as well as the recognition you may receive and the possible career potential for a job well done.

You should take care to stay away from areas of the job where the interviewer may misconstrue your motives for asking. Areas to avoid include benefits, salary, retirement and vacation time. Questions in these areas could put a damper on the interview.

Possible job satisfaction questions could include:

"How does my position here affect the overall goals of the department?"

"If I can learn how to edit on the computerized equipment in the next six months, how will that help the department?"

"What kind of advancement can I expect down the road in this position?"

"What can I do to make a contribution right away to your staff?"

Past Performance Questions

Past performance questions may be the most important to you, particularly if you have reservations about accepting the position. They can prevent you from making a career mistake while promoting yourself with the employer. You are trying to determine what the employer or interviewer feels are the standards of the job. This will expose any unsuspected problems you might face later.

For example, if the last six incumbents left because of job burnout, that might have an effect on whether or not you would accept the position. Similarly, if the last three production assistants advanced up the ladder within the organization, that is a piece of information that might excite you about your prospects in this particular position.

Possible past performance questions are:

"How many people have held the position of editor in the last five years and where are they now?"

"What are some examples of what it takes to give a superior performance in this job?"

"Have any people who held this position left the company? Where did they go?"

Sales Questions

Sales questions help you to understand exactly the kind of person the employer would like to hire and allow you to formulate sales statements promoting your candidacy. By listening carefully to the answers, you will be able to restate your credentials in the terms used by the interviewer. Use his or her terminology when possible because that will make the interviewer comfortable.

Always ask what personality traits the employer desires in his or her employees. You can then put together a sales statement using those terms to describe your personality.

Because there is no such thing as the "perfect candidate" for any job, you may be missing a qualification or two. In such cases, describe an asset you have that makes up for any deficiency you have. The deficiency that the employer perceives may be real or imagined, but the important thing is for you to make a statement compensating for it.

For example, should you lack academic credentials, point out how your work experience makes up for it. If you have never operated a specific type of equipment—a CMX editor, for example—

state that your past experiences editing on a Paltex or other similar editor compensates for it.

If your credentials exceed the qualifications, be certain to point that out. If they are looking for someone who can shoot on remotes and you can light location scenes as well, tell the interviewer.

Possible sales questions include:

"What experience do you require for this job?"
"If you had an ideal candidate, what credentials would he or she possess?"
"What are the educational requirements for the position?"
"Tell me the kind of performance you'd expect to get from an experienced candidate in this position?"

The Most Difficult Question to Ask

The hardest question is part question and part statement. The one thing candidates should cover if they want the job is to ask for it. Asking for the job may be the one thing the employer wants to hear from you. Most candidates lack the confidence to do this.

Because stating that you feel you can do the job and would like to do it for the employer makes you feel insecure, developing a series of questions to lead you into it can break down your reluctance to confront the subject.

As you have seen, the job interview is a sales situation where you are basically marketing yourself. Any good salesperson knows that the one essential ingredient of selling is to ask for the order! In other words, if you want the job, ask for it!

There will be many people who say that this line of questioning is too harsh and may actually lessen your chances of getting the job. But, after interviewing countless candidates and dealing with employers who have interviewed many more, it is refreshing to have a candidate who has the credentials ask for the job. It may be that asking for the job will put you ahead of the many others, equally qualified, who have not.

Simply put, if you do not ask, you probably will not get an offer. But if you show determination and confidence by asking, you may get an offer that was waiting to be had.

The following line of questioning is just to give you an idea of how you can work it into the interview. Like the other questions, it is best to work it out using your own words; however, a possible approach could be, "From all that you've told me, I know that I can do the job for you. I have the background to do the job and I'd like the opportunity to show what I can do. I feel that I'm the best person for the job because of what we've covered. When can I start work for you?"

CONCLUSION

Following these basic rules as well as understanding the employers' views can help you tailor your qualifications to each individual interview. Realize that the hiring decision is not an easy one for the person across the desk from you. Understand that you have to SELL yourself (because if you don't, nobody else will). Do not be self-centered regarding what the job will do for you. Tell the person on the other side of the desk what you can do to benefit the company.

Be able to answer questions regarding yourself, your personality, your motivation for the position and the salary situation.

Tough questions such as why you were terminated or left a job are answerable with proper preparation. This includes practice and dealing with past employers, if necessary. You will realize that termination is not the end of the world as long as you can show you learned from the experience.

Do not forget that asking questions is also an important part of the interview. It is your way to show the interviewer that you are interested in the job and have done your homework on the company.

Your confidence in the entire hiring process, will enable you to move ahead in an exciting and fulfilling career in nonbroadcast video.

7
Resumes, Qualifications Briefs and Resume Reels

In this chapter, we will examine the roles of resumes, qualifications briefs and resume reels in the hiring process. Each is an important tool for finding a job in nonbroadcast video.

Resumes are a necessary evil of the hiring process. While they serve a definite need, they are frequently used to the detriment of job seekers as well. To help you appreciate how and why they are often misused, let us look at resumes from the employers' point of view.

THE UNSOLICITED RESUME

In the past, employers expected a predictable springtime deluge of unsolicited resumes from graduating seniors. Now, resumes cross video managers' desks at an alarming rate throughout the year. The sheer volume of unsolicited resumes often makes it impossible for a video hiring authority to do much more than take a brief look at each one and pitch it into the nearest circular file.

This problem occurs because, until recently, colleges did not teach the practicalities of looking for a job, especially that first job. Also, bookstores are filled with how-to manuals by experts who never seem to agree on how to write a resume.

Most people who have gone the route of sending mass resume mailings will tell you that it is largely a waste of time. The sheer volume of unsolicited resumes that employers receive causes candidates to be qualified out of a job rather than into it.

Successful executive recruiters advise heavily against sending unsolicited resumes—particularly the shotgun approach of sending one to every conceivable company listed in the telephone or business directory.

The reason is simple: People hire people, not paper.

An unsolicited resume is about as welcome as unsolicited junk mail. Most managers try to concentrate on doing what is important and the clutter of "an unasked-for" resume meets its doom quickly. More than likely, it never gets past the secretary who screens out unnecessary correspondence.

Understand that an employer will hire a candidate after conducting an interview, but not from a piece of paper. The stories about a manager reading a resume, rising from his desk, perspiring heavily, shaking with joy and crying to his staff, "Manna from Heaven! This guy's the answer to our prayers! Get him in here!" just do not happen.

A resume is, theoretically, a condensation of all your experiences and wisdom in a quickly readable set of paragraphs. If, however, I am looking for someone with writing experience and I see your unsolicited resume loaded with director credits, I'm likely to drop you from consideration.

You may have terrific writing credentials, but because you did not know what I was looking for, you did not feature it in your resume. Because you did not feature it, I did not know about it, and you did not get the job.

A much better approach than sending unsolicited resumes for jobs that may or may not be available is to first establish a contact list and then qualify the contacts. Try to qualify each one in person. If that is not possible, then do it over the phone. When you are asked to send a resume, determine first whether it is simply a way to get rid of you or if the employer is actually interested in your background.

You can find that out by asking questions. For example, you might say, "Obviously, something I said about my background interested you. What kind of questions do you have, so I can give you more information?" We will cover objections later, but for now, establish whether the employer has a real interest in you. Then, tailor your resume to feature the areas that interest the hiring authority.

Some firms, particularly small ones, *do* read unsolicited resumes, and some people *have* gotten jobs as a result of sending them, so you may still want to consider this route. But, to increase your chances of having your resume read and considered, I suggest, at the very least, that you either contact the organization before you send one, or find out something about the company to determine what the organization does and the positions that might be appropriate for your qualifications.

FEATURES OF A GOOD RESUME

Figures 7.1 and 7.2 are sample resumes. Adrienne Ross' resume (see Figure 7.1) is a typical sample for a person starting a career in nonbroadcast television. Joe Johnson's resume (see Figure 7.2) is more indicative of a veteran of the industry. The bibliography at the end of this book lists some recommended career search books. They contain different methods of resume preparation. While there is not one correct way to write a resume, there are parameters you can follow to increase the usefulness of your resume.

The sample resumes shown here are designed to *work* for each candidate. Rather than just list experiences, these resumes accentuate the candidate's positive features and benefits. While looking them over, note some of the features of each resume.

Contents of a Good Resume

First Person

Both candidates have, for the most part, eliminated the use of "I" in the body of the resume. Never use Mr., Mrs. or Ms. either.

Figure 7.1: Sample Resume for a Newcomer to the Nonbroadcast Video Industry

ADRIENNE ROSS
334 Oak Brook Lane
Oakland, California 98892
213-555-9003

EDUCATION

M.A.: TV Production—University of Southern California—1988

B.S.: Radio & TV—University of Southern California—1986—Dean's List

EXPERIENCE

1986-1988

UNIVERSITY OF SOUTHERN CALIFORNIA
Department of TV Production

Teaching Assistant

Responsibilities included teaching of two television production classes per quarter and supervising student-operated cable channel. Instituted new programming that expanded student viewership by 75%. Operated all studio and remote equipment and directed or produced over 100 programs per quarter.

Coursework included: advanced directing and production, corporate video and television management. Received an ITVA Golden Reel Award for production.

1983-1986

UNIVERSITY OF SOUTHERN CALIFORNIA
Learning Resource Center

Production Assistant

Responsibilities included delivery of educational audiovisual materials and production of instructional

**Figure 7.1: Sample Resume for a Newcomer to the
Nonbroadcast Video Industry (Cont.)**

television programs. Promoted to campus night supervisor.

Radio & TV Department

Student

Coursework included: television and radio production, public speaking, business management, accounting and data processing.

Summers
1982–1986

COX CABLE TV

Volunteer

Assisted on television productions including local origination, educational funding marathons and local news programs. Produced, wrote and edited the community news program that included coverage of city council meetings, interviews with local politicians, and coverage of local parades, community gatherings and events.

The Objective

Neither resume has one. Objectives can be too confining. Sometimes you should use an objective to target a certain job, but doing so can restrict your opportunities for other jobs. For example, an objective that states your desire to manage can be taken to mean that any position that has no supervisory duties is of no interest to you. That may not be the case.

Figure 7.2: Sample Resume for an Advanced Position in Nonbroadcast Video

JOE JOHNSON
1155 East 12th Street
Atlanta, GA 30339
404-555-0673

EXPERIENCE

1983-Present

INTERNATIONAL DOODAT CORPORATION
Division of IDC, Inc.
Largest producer of semisoft doodats in the world.

Production Supervisor

Responsible for all scheduling of productions, equipment and staff, directing of major programs, supervising of production staff; producer on all management–related programs, assisted producers on all other
programs. Have good knowledge of 1-inch computer
editing and graphics systems. Assist in hiring and coordination of projects with the department.

The video department has operated at only a 5% increase in cost over the past five years while the
number of productions has increased by 47%. The
company noted this in its last annual report to the
parent company as an example of good management.

1980-1983

JONES, CARROWTHERS, AND FLINTSMITH
Accountants—9th largest in the United States.

Producer/Director

Started a newsmagazine program for the firm's 13,000
employees that was so successful 10 other firms con-
sulted with us to start their own. Three awards,

Figure 7.2: Sample Resume for an Advanced Position
in Nonbroadcast Video (Cont.)

including IABC Silver Quill. Resulted in promotion to Producer/Director.

Produced and directed all programs, including videotape and live programs for training, employee and client information, project proposal programs, satellite videoconference training, studio productions, remote recordings, large audience productions and screenings.

1977–1980   **EDUCOM, INC.**
One of the largest textbook publishers in the United States.

Editor

Started the video department as an adjunct to textbook sales. Produced programs in conjunction with the sales division to boost sales to vendors. Responsible for all editing. Sales in textbook division climbed by 35% as a direct result of this program series. Promoted from Production Assistant to Editor.

EDUCATION   B.S.: Telecommunications—1976—University of Michigan. Graduated in top 10% of class.

PROFESSIONAL   International Association of Business Communicators
AFFILIATIONS   International Television Association
International Teleconferencing Association

PERSONAL   Birth Date: June 10, 1954.   Married, 3 children.
In excellent health.

COMMENTS   I enjoy the challenge of information management and quickly undertake new projects. I get along well with my peers and am responsive to top management's needs. I am willing to relocate.

General Look

Both resumes contain lots of white space. Neither appears crowded. An uncluttered resume invites people to read it. Also, notice that the resumes are brief. Long resumes are rarely read and sometimes make the employer feel that you are making up in quantity what you lack in quality.

Personal Data

Age and sex have no bearing. Marital status is used only on the tenured person's resume and then only because it can be shown to be of benefit. (Employers often feel that marriage is an indication of stability.) All other personal data is, at least in theory, not applicable. For example, superfluous information such as hobbies should be left out. On a good resume, personal information should be limited to two lines.

Professional Affiliations

These are not memberships, such as travel clubs. A student of mine insisted on placing her "Star Trekker" membership on her resume. Her logic was that other Trekkers would see it and therefore increase her chances of being "beamed up," but it seemed silly to me. Professional affiliations should relate to the industry.

Education

On Adrienne's resume, education leads because it is the most important and recent experience she has had. Notice the emphasis is on actual experience and that her coursework is given some, but not much weight. Television production courses are not regarded as highly practical experience.

On advanced resumes like Joe's, mention your education in a quiet way. A degree that is 15 years old is not a real benefit to an employer, but lack of one can be a knockout factor. Candidates with multiple degrees should list the most recent one first.

Work Experience

Like education, it should be listed with the most recent experience leading. Adrienne's entry-level resume shows pertinent summer jobs. Other part-time jobs that have relevance to the job you are seeking can be added as well.

Joe did not include jobs while in school on his advanced resume. The resume must show what you did for each organization. Salaries are not necessary on resumes, nor are reasons for leaving. But, as stated earlier, you should plan for discussion of these topics *during* the interview.

Using FAB in Your Resume

It is best to think about what you accomplished in your background when creating your resume. Then, using the FAB technique described in Chapter 4, state what you have done with the benefit aimed to the employer. If you are having trouble organizing your work experience information, think about answering questions like these:

- While I was there I supervised . . .
- I created, wrote, produced, directed, edited, shot . . .
- I established, organized or built . . .
- I saved the organization . . .
- My changes to the system were . . .
- Because of me, the department was able to . . .

Now, take each position and describe what you did. Those are your *features* for the position. What you specifically did in each experience are your *accomplishments*. And the *benefits* are the following words for you to convey in person to the employer: "... and I can do the same for you." Write and rewrite these descriptions and use action words with positive connotations as often as possible.

Words with positive connotations create an upbeat atmosphere about yourself. Some of these words include: *administered, completed, built, produced, expanded, improved, promoted, organized, responsible, set up, led, increased, directed, started, paid, success, instituted, climbed, challenged.*

Check how many of these positive action words are included in both Adrienne's and Joe's resumes. And then see how many are in yours. The thesaurus can help you with many more.

NONBROADCAST TELEVISION RESUME
DOS AND DON'TS

Some additional caveats apply to resumes in the nonbroadcast television industry:

- The best results come from tailored, not mass-produced resumes. Because of the many different fields that comprise the industry and the variety of needs of various departments, each position in nonbroadcast video is different. What a producer is to one person means a writer/director to another. Find out what a specific position requires and feature the experiences in your background that match those requirements.

- Copier–produced resumes look like everyone in the industry is receiving one. If possible, type or use a word processor to produce your resume. Recently, an out-of-town producer who wanted to move back to the Midwest sent me a very nice resume, cover letter and resume reel. Shortly after the interview I found out that almost everyone else in the local ITVA chapter received the same package. Although it may have been effective, the "mass–produced job search" aspects left a sour taste in my mouth.

- While "tailoring" the resume may not be possible in the early stages of your hunt, a compromise would be to write a more directed resume for interviews that are for specific jobs. Keep a resume "template" and plug in what you need according to the position you seek. The benefit to the employer is he/she can see immediately that your experience fits the job. The benefit to you is that you can emphasize the areas of your work history that relate to the position and de-emphasize the rest.

- Avoid trendy or unusual typefaces or colored paper stock. What they say about you as a person may not be what you intended. Of late, it seems that rose or purple is favored by women, while men are still stuck on goldenrod or salmon. A man looking for an entry-level position called me recently after sending me a note with his resume and explained that he felt trendy-looking resumes showed the real creativity of the person. He saw no correlation between his offbeat resume fonts and people's reluctance to interview him.

- Keep your resume short and to the point. The first page gets read, the second one gets looked at, the third and beyond are forgotten.

- Never, never, never send copies of your final report card, facsimiles of your degrees or awards or letters of recommendation with your resume.

- Job descriptions that are unclear should be briefly explained. Example: "I studio-directed 14 different productions, while field-directing 20. The studio shoots involved crews of up to 15, while I generally used a two-person field crew."

- Do not put equipment model numbers on your resume. The only possible exception might be experience with a unique piece. Should it be important for you to be able to operate certain types of video equipment, that information can be covered in the interview using the *qualifications brief*, which will be explained later in this chapter. Video equipment changes so rapidly that using model numbers can date your experience. If you say you can operate the Sony DXC-1800 camera and the employer knows that they have not been produced in 10 years, your background appears dated.

- Try not to have a resume that looks like Superman's. This can be a problem because in nonbroadcast video, people often wear many hats. Therefore, they often have knowledge of several positions that can be careers by themselves. To avoid the superhuman appearance, try to concentrate your resume on certain areas in which you have extensive expertise. A person who looks like he or she can do anything can be viewed suspiciously by employers who think the job applicant is too good to be true.

- Use FAB liberally. If you were a writer for a company, quantify what you did and explain, in percentages if possible, the effect your writing had on the company.

- Be concerned if you have too many jobs on your resume. It may appear that you are a job hopper or job shopper. If you held several jobs within one organization, make mention of this achievement, but under one heading. Emphasize the similarities of the positions. Try to tie two or more positions together, so that they appear to be, in essence, the same "job" in different organizations. If you have had many jobs, prepare to handle it in a positive light. Try not to blame anyone for your many job changes. However, do not conveniently "forget" jobs. If a job you held is not mentioned and you are "found out," your credibility will take a beating.

- Dates are necessary, but should not be too obtrusive. You should list the year of your final degree and the years you worked in each position. Functional resumes without dates tip off the employer that you are trying to hide something, such as a lack of current experience. Honesty is the best policy when looking for a job. Your integrity is of great importance. Today, more than ever before, employers want to have employees who are honest.

- References are not necessary for the resume. You can provide them when you interview. Also, you can burn any letters of recommendation. Most employers are sophisticated enough not to believe them and know that they are often written by the candidate and signed by the former boss. (Mine were.)

After you have written and rewritten your resume and tried to condense it as much as possible, play devil's advocate with yourself. Go through your resume and see what is actually needed and what is superfluous. Rewrite it and this time ask for a critique from someone whose judgment you value. A friend in the industry will be of most help. Ask for honest criticism and edit your resume accordingly. Only then might your resume be ready for your search.

Resumes are necessary to the job hunt. While they can be used to screen you out, persistent questioning of the employer coupled with targeted FAB experiences should get you into an interview. That is the purpose of resumes.

THE QUALIFICATIONS BRIEF

While the resume provides a fine overview of your capabilities, you can display your background more deeply with a qualifications brief. The qualifications brief allows you to expand your resume. It also serves as a written guide from which you can work in the interview and gives additional support to your presentation. The brief should be used during the interview to provide the "visualization" of your career.

The brief should tell not only what you have experienced, but how well you have done things in your past and what you have accomplished. It should be written clearly and efficiently; it should get to the point. It is an inventory of your work history and education and is meant to help people who do not know anything about you to learn great things about you in a brief time. The brief, like the resume, must be written, rewritten, edited and polished. While you should keep the resume brief, the qualifications brief can be more elaborate.

Preparing the Qualifications Brief

Complete one sheet for every job you have held. If you are fresh from college, list summer and part-time positions as well. At the top of the sheet state your name, then write your job title, the company you worked for and the dates you held the position.

Divide the paper into two separate columns. On the left side list the duties and responsibilities of the job. At the bottom left, you should state the supervisor's name, job title, and the salary at which you started the job. List only one job per sheet. If you were promoted to a new position, make out a new sheet for each new position.

The same process is appropriate for education. Prepare a qualifications sheet for each college you attended. On the left side list courses you took as well as extracurricular activities. Obviously, your work at the campus radio or TV station should be listed as an example of practical experience. But even work outside your main concentration of study should be taken into account.

Perhaps the crisis intervention work you did as a part of your sociology courses will give you the edge in a company looking for someone to write, produce and promote specialized employee relations programs. Also, it may enhance your qualifications in dealing with healthcare facilities or governmentally funded intervention programs.

Be specific at all times. Use percentages to back up your claims when possible. Use terms that are descriptive and leave no doubt as to their meaning.

Employment History Qualifications Brief

Figure 7.3 is a sample qualifications brief for a job candidate who started the video department and built it from ground zero to its present four people and $500,000 in video equipment. The department's annual budget is $250,000. The brief includes a short statement about the applicant's responsibilities and accomplishments.

Figure 7.3: Qualifications Brief #1:
Employment History

Director of Video Productions	MANAGEMENT RECRUITERS INTERNATIONAL INC.	July, 1981– Present

DUTIES & RESPONSIBILITIES

PERFORMANCE

Started department and built it from ground zero to its present four-person complement with over $500,000 in video equipment and $1 million in facilities. Supervised the building of the state-of-the-art studio. Responsible for all hiring, training of personnel, meeting with clients, program development, pre-production through to post-production. Coordinated complete distribution of tape network to over 550 offices nationwide. Produced 70 programs each year.

Formulated plan to have department produce for outside clients, thereby lessening the need of the department to assess all costs to main corporate parent. In three years, department has surpassed projections by 20%. Department is self-sustaining and has increased production in three years by 10% without hiring additional personnel. Unit produces 60% in-house; 40% for out-of-house clients.

Starting salary: $22,500

Presently earning: $49,500

Reason for leaving: Seek new challenges

Educational Background Qualifications Brief

The qualifications brief presented in Figure 7.4 emphasizes educational background because the applicant is a relative new-comer to nonbroadcast video. While a college student, the applicant started as a volunteer for a college-owned nightclub and eventually moved up through the ranks to manage a 20-person volunteer staff that produced weekly live entertainment shows for students.

As you can see in these qualifications briefs, this is not the time to be modest. State the facts honestly. If you did something and did it well, say so. If you did not do it and are tempted to

Figure 7.4: Qualifications Brief #2:
Educational Background

Master of Arts		
School of Speech	Kent State University	1971–1973
Telecommunications	Kent, OH	

Major: Television Production	Degree & date: M.A. August, 1973
Minor: Business Management	Major GPA: 3.2 (4.0)
Other Courses: Photography Speech	Overall GPA: 3.2 (4.0)
Extracurricular Activities: Graduate assistant for television production courses; ran two labs per week. Managed the campus cable TV station, TV-2, three nights per week.	Completed a written production project for master's thesis. Earned money to pay 100% of college expenses.

indicate that you did, do not lie. Remember, use the FAB plan as much as possible.

At the bottom of each sheet, list your personal references. Also, in a positive light, state your reasons for leaving your current job.

On the right side of the educational sheets, list substantiation, such as degrees earned (date and title), honors, scholarships, grade point average, the percent of college expenses you paid on your own and the results and benefits of your extracurricular activities.

Obviously, education has great meaning to a potential employer if it is in the immediate past. As I indicated earlier, the details of your educational background tend to fade in importance as you move along with your career. Fifteen years ago I received my master's degree in television; today I rarely count it as experience. Just too many years have gone by.

The Miscellaneous Qualifications Brief

Develop a miscellaneous qualifications sheet. (See Figure 7.5.) This sheet inventories the balance of your career-related activities

Figure 7.5: Qualifications Brief #3:
Miscellaneous Accomplishments

DUTIES AND RESPONSIBILITIES

Volunteer for college-owned nightclub. Moved up eventually to manage club and 20-person staff. By learning management and entertainment techniques, I was able to increase attendance at club by over 400% in two years.

PERFORMANCE

Because of this success, I became responsible for large entertainment concerts. This culminated in the long-range planning and execution of a music festival that attracted more than 35,000 people over two nights of concerts. Received letters from faculty advisor and academic vice–president praising organization of festival.

that have not appeared on any other sheet. This should include volunteer work, student jobs, hobbies, workshops, seminars or conventions you have attended and any other outside interests that qualify you for the position.

The right side is reserved for you to evaluate your performance. Often, it is the most troublesome part. We tend to think of the job we did, but are often too modest to relate how well we did it. Now you need to "sell" yourself. Think about what you accomplished while in each position.

List performance indicators, such as promotions, salary increases and written and oral praise received from your superiors or clients. Accomplishments you should include are scripts and the number and types of productions you assisted, scheduling methods or production techniques you introduced, programs you participated in that saved time or money, speeches or seminars you gave, results, profits, series, special reports and ideas you initiated.

If you were in a managerial position, it is appropriate to include the accomplishments of your subordinates.

THE RESUME REEL

The resume reel, or videotape, helps you confirm the competency you have claimed in your written resume and interview. It is a visual and aural showcasing of the programs you have contributed to and a glowing testimony to what you have accomplished.

In this respect, television is a unique profession. Only in television can you demonstrate an exact record of your professional experiences. On a resume reel you can show exactly what you participated in and specifically what contribution you made. It is an exciting tool that, when used correctly, can add dramatic impact to your search.

More than anything else, the resume reel can clinch the job or eliminate you from consideration. It is your way of saying "I can do the job because I did it here and here and . . . ."

Employers tell me that, like resumes, resume reels *do* weed out people. Keep that in mind when you put yours together. It should not be slapped together with any less consideration than you would put together your resume or brief. Like your brief, it allows you to visualize your achievements and benefits for the potential employer. While the brief is your written accompaniment, the resume reel is further proof of your credentials.

Talent have found the use of resume reels to be invaluable. Most producers will not hire talent unless they have seen them on tape first. If you are short on camera credits, get together with a production facility or freelance producer to put a resume reel together. For talent, variety is the key. Besides commercials, you should have extemporaneous interviews, news anchoring stints and various straight or character role parts from training or other communications programs. If you are working already, make it a point to ask for a copy of your work from the production. Most nonbroadcast television personnel are happy to oblige. Carry extra tapes with you to the shoots for that purpose.

For all nonbroadcast personnel, the resume reel provides vivid documentation of what you have done and what you are capable of doing. It allows a prospective employer to look into the future and "see" what you can do for him or her.

Resume Reel Dos and Don'ts

- Make it short and to the point. In the first five minutes you should have demonstrated your various skills in a variety of programs. Try to keep each segment under a minute. Use character generation to clearly label and explain each sequence before it appears. The cassette and cover box should carry a list of what is on the tape with segment title and length.
- If, after the first five to seven minutes, you wish to add a more expanded segment, go ahead. Expanded segments should be something unusual or inherently exciting. For example, one freelance producer brought in a reel that showed a few segments of a massive teleconference he

had produced. It whetted my appetite. Then, after the rest of his five minutes rolled, he offered to show me more of the conference that "just happened" to be on the rest of the tape. The cold and cruel reality of resume reels is that only a few minutes of your experiences may be viewed. But having readily available expanded segments may come in handy.

- If you have a variety of skills, show them. Multitalented individuals usually break the tape into segments. One segment shows editing skills. A second segment shows your camera skills. A third shows your directing talents. And a fourth represents a program you produced from script to finished product.

- Writers can also benefit by using a resume reel. A writer once sent me a 30-page script as evidence of her expertise. While I could ascertain that she had a distinct style, the reality is that most employers will not spend much time looking at a script. However, they *will* look at the tape of the production. If it is unique and interesting, your script in "living" form can help you even more.

- Should you feel that an expanded explanation of your involvement is necessary, enclose a list inside the tape box of what is on the reel and what you did. If you ran the second camera, say so (e.g., all shots from stage right were my camera). Say whether you edited, wrote, shot or directed the project.

- Never show something you did not do. If you are hired and told to "Edit it like that program you showed us," you are sunk. Nor should you include a program that you made a minor contribution to. Two different producers showed me segments on their tapes that, after questioning, they admitted they had very little to do with. A similar thing happened in Pittsburgh. An aspiring videographer "borrowed" some shots to spice up his reel. An employer viewing the reel discovered the inaccuracies, reported the infringement, and a nasty scene with the real owners ensued.

- Do not get hung up showing the beginning of a program. If the attention-getting segment is in the body of the program, start at that point. If you are showing the tape to people who are in the industry, they do not need to start at the beginning.

- Pick things that show off your handiwork, but to be sure, have it reviewed first by a friend in the industry.

- MTV has made a tremendous impact on the youth of America, but nonbroadcast video employers will not be excited about your music video. Music videos rarely have objectives other than entertainment; they do not mean very much in nonbroadcast television. It's better to display your expertise in the conventional formats that employers would use themselves (i.e., training, news or how-to programs).

- Similarly, network news, sporting events and motion pictures make uneventful viewing for the nonbroadcast executive. One reason these do not impress employers in this industry is because most broadcast projects require 20 to 100 people in different positions. Therefore, it is almost impossible to get a clear impression of the applicant's skills from a production worked on by so many. Large nonbroadcast productions have similar problems. A friend of mine showed me a 26-minute state lottery association program that cost $90,000 to produce. While he *did* produce it, it was difficult from all the expensive visuals and multiple shoots to determine exactly what he did and what others did. A 30-minute program with a budget of $100,000 may use as many as 25 different people in a variety of production capacities. While most ENG crews are two or three people, studio productions, like the news, can take anywhere from 10 to 40 people to produce, depending on the size of the market and station.

- Productions should clearly show your professionalism. A small two-person remote production will showcase your talents by making your contribution easily recognizable.
- Just as with resumes, I do not recommend sending a tape without at least an in-depth phone interview. I understand employers' reluctance to fly you cross-country for an interview before they have viewed a reel of your work. And that's okay. But sending tapes to "blind box number" advertisements or to possible employers you have had little or no actual contact with is not worth the postage.
- Prepare to duplicate your tape in different formats. Ask what format the employer wants your videotape in. Showing up with a Beta videotape when all they have is VHS is embarrassing, to say the least. Retain a clean master on a 1-inch or 3/4-inch format for dubbing purposes. If you do not get the position, you can immediately dub copies off the master to send elsewhere.
- Never put yourself in the position of having to ask an employer to hurry with a tape so you can send it elsewhere. The employer will think that you are jumping from place to place for a job (which may, indeed, be the case, but do not let it appear to be the case). Making several dubs is easy. Any local production facility should be able to tell you whom to call.
- Stay flexible in putting together your reel. It may need updating from time to time in order to showcase recent jobs. Keep the quality of your reel high.
- Freelancers who want to move into full-time employment should keep copies of their latest experiences for inclusion on their tapes.

The resume reel is your portfolio. It explains what you have done and how you did it. And it provides visual proof to back up your claims regarding your experiences. It should represent your best—like your resume and qualifications brief. And you should put a great deal of thought into it—just like your resume and brief.

CONCLUSION

Now that you have prepared the resume, the qualifications brief and the resume reel, you are still not ready for the interview. Commit the information to memory so that you can talk easily and thoroughly with an air of authority. It is your life. You should know the most about it and should be able to talk about it to the employer when the time comes. And when you are fielding questions about your background, you should be able to easily point out the qualifications in your background that match the job you are seeking.

These three tools—the resume, the qualifications brief and the resume reel—are your visual aids to help sell yourself to the employer. Their quality says more about you than anything else, except you.

8
Finding a New Job

Each year millions of Americans look for a new job. The reasons they give are varied, but the central theme is the same: either they do not like what they do and want to look elsewhere or they have to look because their job, for one reason or another, is going to end. While a new job is not always the cure to job problems, there is a right way and wrong way to go about looking for a new job.

If you are already employed, do not plan on quitting to devote all your time to finding a new job. Unless you are independently wealthy, the lack of income will eventually have a negative impact on your job hunt. And, you are in a much stronger position when you are already employed.

Staying with your present job while you search for a new position not only keeps the money coming in, it also puts you in a better position to negotiate job offers. If you are unemployed the employer will think that you are desperate for a job and that he or she can call the shots. Not having a job can dictate how good the offer looks to you. By being employed, you can make a more realistic assessment of a job offer. In addition, you are doing the job now for someone else. That kind of subtle message can get you a better offer.

The search can be a thankless job. Chances are, you will get a lot of rejections and a fair amount of "almost, but no cigar" results. Although your friends and family may lend support, you will be alone on the front lines. You will get rejected and you will have to pull yourself up by the bootstraps and try again and again.

There are no shortcuts and no excuses for stalling. If the interview is at 9:00 A.M. on Tuesday, you are going to have to present your best at that time. If no interviews are scheduled and you have run out of contacts, it will be up to you to decide who to call next, what to say and where to network to find new sources of available jobs.

And, once you do everything right and a job you have interviewed for is offered, it will be you and only you who will have to decide whether it really is better than what you have now.

THE COSTS OF FINDING A JOB

Looking for another job, be it entry-level or higher, is actually a full-time job that can easily take over 40 hours a week and will eat up vacation time while you search. It will greatly lessen your available personal time.

A lateral move, such as an editor moving to another editor position with very little or no pay increase, takes about two months (based on hiring standards for all industry). If you are making a move with a salary increase, expect it to take as long as six months.[1]

If you are earning $24,000 a year and quit, you can expect to take a $4,000 to $12,000 loss over a two- to six-month period of unemployment. You should also figure about 20% more for loss in benefits, if you are unemployed during this time. Money is also required for phone calls, resume preparation and printing, new clothes and travel.

ASSESSING YOUR CAREER

While there are not any hard or fast rules as to when you should look for a new position, there are some signs you can read that will indicate that it is time for a change.

---

[1] Robert Half, *The Robert Half Way to Get Hired in Today's Job Market* (NY: Rawson, Wade, 1981), pp. 41–43.

Is your current position the one that you want to be in at this time in your career? Can you see yourself in this job five years from now, 10 years from now?

Where can you grow (go) from your job? Are there other duties and areas of responsibilities that you can add that would enhance your career with your present employer? What kinds of further education and experience do you need to improve your chances of receiving additional duties and responsibilities?

If there is not enough opportunity for growth within your current organization, what positions do you know of outside your organization that would be interesting and challenging? What is the growth potential of those positions? What do you intend to learn from those positions to help you in your career?

In your present job, how do you relate to the people you work with? Your peers? Your bosses? Are you receiving recognition, promotions and bonuses commensurate with others on a similar level? Or are you being passed up? Why? What can you do about it?

What are your goals in life? What do you have to do to achieve your goals? As each position you hold is a stepping stone to your career goals, how does your current position fit? How does the next position you intend to seek fit in with your goal?

What can you do to eliminate dissatisfaction in your job? Are you challenged enough in your position? If not, what can be done to provide more challenges and opportunities?

What are you qualified to do? What would be the position titles? Where would you look? How much of your current compensation is organizationally related? That is, how much are you paid because of your own knowledge of the organization? How much of that knowledge is transferable to a new employer? How can what you have learned so far in your career benefit another organization? What specifically can you do to help another organization?

Enhancing Your Present Position

You might notice, from the above questions, that I put a great deal of emphasis on how you can enhance your career at your current job. There are two reasons for this. One, you already have the job. If other duties or responsibilities can be added to your present position to enhance it, it would be easier to move laterally or upward within your own organization than to go through the time and expense of looking elsewhere. Most bosses would love their subordinates to ask for more work.

In a successful economy, personnel consultants have found it harder to get qualified candidates for jobs than job orders for position openings. A head of a large western post-production facility lamented the difficulty he had in filling a third editor's spot: "The job has been open over six months now. I'm pulling my hair out because we can't find someone. Either they don't have the CMX editing experience we need or they have the qualifications, but don't want to move to another job. And their employers are making it so they don't *want* to leave!!"

Second, by deciding to go outside without considering all possible opportunities within your present organization, you may become vulnerable to a sticky situation. When you walk in to resign your boss may wish you the best. Or he may tell you to get out immediately. Or he may try to buy some time with the oldest technique in the book: the counteroffer.

Never Accept a Counteroffer

The counteroffer is an attempt by your present employer to keep you from moving to another concern by countering the offer of the new position. The offer can take a number of different shapes. Your boss may say to you:

- "I should have told you sooner, it's my fault that we haven't—we have plans for you that will come to fruition within 30 to 90 days."

- "We'll match that offer you received and better it by (X) percent. This raise was supposed to go into effect by the first part of next quarter, but because of your fine record with us, and the fact that we want to keep you, we're giving you the raise earlier."
- "I shouldn't be doing this, but I'm going to let you in on some confidential information. We're in the process of reorganizing the division and we have plans that will give you a significant promotion within the next two months."
- "When I told my boss of your decision, he told me he wants to meet with you and your spouse over dinner as soon as possible. Just let me know when, and he'll drop everything to discuss this with you."

What is really happening with the counteroffer is that your present employer is buying time until he or she can get rid of you on the employer's terms. Employment industry surveys have found that 80% of all people who accept a counteroffer are gone from that company within a year. When you quit, it is on your terms. You picked the time, you picked the place. Later, after your boss has had time to react to your desire to leave, plans can be made to replace you on his or her terms.

In today's business climate, the loyalty of employers and employees is not as strong as it once was. When times get tough, companies cut back or lay off. It is as simple as that. And if you should find greener pastures elsewhere, then you should feel as much loyalty to the company as the company does to you. And don't look back.

When being presented with a counteroffer, think with your head, not your heart. It can be very flattering to receive one. The emotions of leaving a job might influence you. The prospect of a new job could fill you with the fear of the unknown. In fact you may find that a strong case of buyer's remorse may set in. Don't let it!

A good way to deal with the emotions that the counteroffer evokes is to see if you will always say "no" to the following questions. (A "yes" answer to any question means that you should not consider the counteroffer.)

1. Did I decide to change jobs because I felt a new position would offer me greater opportunity?
2. If I stay here, will my loyalty to the organization always be suspect?
3. If my loyalty is questioned, did I just move myself up the line to be terminated if a recession or downturn occurs?
4. Is the offered raise just my annual review coming early?
5. If I'm staying in the same position but being paid above the norm, could this be a simple time-buying ploy to find someone to take my job at lower pay?
6. Do I have to threaten to resign every time I want a raise or to advance in my career?

Once you have made the decision to leave, try to keep everything logical and free from emotion. Write a letter to your present employer explaining your intentions and thanking him or her for the experience. Keep the ending of your job professional. You never know when that good will might be needed later in life.

Give the standard two-week notice; your new employer should not be kept waiting. Look upon the counteroffer as a belated confirmation of the contributions you have made. Keep your eye on your goal and continue to move ahead in your career. If you do not decide what is best for you, who else will?

LOOKING-FOR-A-JOB (LFAJ) AXIOMS

Once you have made the decision to look for a new job, there are 10 important rules to keep in mind.

LFAJ Axiom #1: Jobs Are Frequently Created at the Interview

Approximately 40% of all jobs are created at an interview. You can increase your chances of landing a position at an interview by making favorable impressions on people who *can* offer you a position. Many hiring authorities will candidly tell you that there are people they have hired because they felt that "this is the kind of person we want here."

This alone illustrates the power of gathering contacts and preparing for the interview. An employer may have a certain position open, but meet with someone who may not have exactly the right qualifications. The employer may feel "sold" on the individual and restructure an assignment because he or she feels that the person will be a valuable asset in spite of any deficiencies.

In television it is very important to be a part of a team. During an interview for a job you are trying to show the employer that you would fit well on his or her team. That is, you are the missing part of the puzzle. If the employer likes you and feels your background can be of benefit, he/she may structure a job for you (borrowing from one person's responsibilities, adding to another's) just to include you on the team.

One reason this practice is accepted today is that it has been realized, of late, that good management practices involve intuition or "the playing of one's hunches." The intuitive manager is one who has a sixth sense of what is going on and reacts accordingly. Because of this emphasis, employers are apt to play their hunches and hire someone whom they think will fit in and add to the organization somewhere along the line.

LFAJ Axiom #2: Set Up Your Own List of Contacts, Starting With Friends and Relatives

I have talked with a lot of people who are starting to look for a position. After I ascertain what direction they want their careers to take, I ask them who they know and which of those people they can contact to begin their job search.

When you start to look for a new job, contacts are the name of the game. Anything you can do to increase the number of people you know who know you and discreetly know you are looking (translation: not apt to tell your boss) will heighten your chances of finding a suitable job.

Many people tell me, "If only I'd been at the right place at the right time, I'd have gotten that job. It's perfect for me." By increasing contacts you will be increasing your chances of being at the right place at the right time. And, once you get the contact and set up a meeting, there are other ways to increase your chances.

I have found that most people are astonished when I tell them to check with friends and relatives and then to broaden their search from there. Some have actually said something like, "Oh, I couldn't do that . . . I couldn't ask them for a job!" Yet, you have to start somewhere, so I recommend contacting people you know and are comfortable with who might be able to help or even set up a "courtesy" interview.

If you are offered a courtesy interview, that is, one where there is not a position open, but the interview is being conducted as a courtesy to a mutual friend or relative, then go in and interview just as if it were a "real" interview.

Why?

First, you can expand your contact base by selling yourself to the interviewer. He/she may know of a job or other contacts you can call. Always ask all contacts, "Is there anyone else you know who I might talk to or who may have a need for someone with my skills and expertise?" If the interviewer is sold on you then he/she should be interested enough to help someone else who may have a need.

Second, you never know when a job will open unexpectedly with the person performing the courtesy. He/she may be sufficiently impressed and remember you down the road. Remember, 40% of all jobs are created at the interview.

Annie J. is the best administrative assistant a video, print and graphics director could have. I know that because she worked with me for four years. I first met AJ, as she's known, while I was teaching a class in corporate television at John Carroll University in University Heights, OH. I had 30 students who met twice a week and, while most of them did not make much of an impression, a few did. AJ was a hard worker, who seemed genuinely interested. As soon as she was graduated, however, she returned to Dallas to join her parents.

A year or so later, while crossing a busy intersection during a driving rainstorm, who should I run into but AJ. She was working as a temporary secretary for a local bank. We traded stories, and she explained what she had been doing. Although I had always been favorably impressed by her drive and intelligence, I did not have an opening, so I filed her number away and later transferred it to my "contact file."

Two months later, my administrative assistant resigned to move on to a production assistant's position with a large company. I called AJ, and she rode herd on our department for four years. As I said, you never know what might happen "down the road."

LFAJ Axiom #3: Employers Hire People
Through Personal Contacts

Seventy percent of people hired came to the employer's attention via personal contacts.[2] In other words, networking fills more than two thirds of the positions available in industry today.

Personal contacts are not everything in finding a job, but they are close. And in a highly technical industry like nonbroadcast television, which is also "tightly knit," personal contacts are extremely important.

Anyone you may have heard about should be considered a potential job lead. Take your personal address and phone lists

---

[2] William Morris and James Caberra, *How to Survive the Loss of a Job and Find Another Successfully* (Orlando, FL: Harcourt Brace Jovanovich, 1987).

and compile a written list. Start with people you know. They may offer you a job, or they may refer you to someone who may offer you a job or at least an interview (even a courtesy one), or they might tell you of an opening they know about.

LFAJ Axiom #4: Contact Everyone and Completely
Follow Through on Each and Every Lead, Meet With
as Many People Who Might Hire You as Possible

As I stated earlier, people hire people, not paper, so be prepared to interview with as many people as possible. And follow up on every contact you make.

Phil Stella, manager of corporate communications for the Progressive Insurance Company, used the method of contacts and follow-through. When Phil wanted to change from the video teaching profession after 12 years, he followed through on everyone he talked to. While Phil continued to teach, he spent over two years searching, interviewing, talking to contacts, meeting with potential employers and following up on everyone. His efforts paid off. Phil explains the process:

> There are two basic secrets to moving your career upward in this industry. One is the ability to be persistent without being obnoxious. Like a salesman, you have to talk, discuss, cajole, check in and say hello to everyone who might be able to help you. And it can be difficult because everyone has a different level of tolerance. So you have to find that line and push it, but don't cross it.
>
> Next, you need to acknowledge the contributions of your "key contacts" as your job search progresses. You need to call them every six weeks or so and thank them. You should send thank-you notes and write follow-up letters that let them know that you appreciate their help.
>
> You need to take these contacts to lunch now and then. In fact, you need to do anything that can make you conspicuously different in a positive sense. That difference will set you apart and get you ahead.

Phil should know about being different. Later, he helped others because he had not forgotten the people who helped him during his search.

> Once you land, it's important for you to maintain those relationships you built while you were looking. Let them know you appreciate their good advice. Keep the contact networks alive. Remember, you never know when you may need their help again.
> Also, understand that once you find a position, those people can never be repaid for their help. The best thing to do in this industry is to pass it along—you'll become a source for other people looking for a career change.

A turning point in my career came when I first met Derrill Dalby. I was 27, married, owned a house and had car payments to make. I wanted to get into the nonbroadcast field on a permanent basis. I had had a few limited forays into it as well as my radio sales background, but for the most part I had been picking up experience in sales and management.

I still have the contact sheets I used in that ultimately successful canvassing. Contact sheets are an important tool for your job search. They should include the contact's name, telephone number and company affiliation. Keep notes on the sheet about the results of contacting the individual. (For an example of a contact sheet, see Figure 8.1.) It is also a good idea to save these written records for your permanent files. Old contact sheets can become important again for future job searches.

In my search for potential jobs, I called several friends and then several companies that I thought might be large enough to support an audiovisual department. (In 1976, corporate video was still in its infancy.) I started calling colleges after I had determined that one salable point I had was my teaching experience at Kent State University. I had taught the laboratory sections of several

Figure 8.1: Sample Contact Sheet

	Type of Call	Company	Phone Number	Contact	Result/Next Step
1	Referral from Uncle Louie	AB Steel, Inc.	333-3330	Joe Gordon, Dir. of Comm.	Not hiring, but I think he's interested. Stay in touch. Call in 2 weeks.
2	Met at ITVA meeting	Cinecraft Productions	228-9888	Larry Linfeld, Producer	Send a resume. Hires freelancers on an "as needed" basis.
3	Saw in news-paper about expansion	Ramco Ind.	360-9554	Geraldine Laughtner, Vid. Prod. Dir.	Possible prod. asst. opening in 6 months. Call next month.
4	Referral from John Thomas, Intep Tape Products	Starlight Video	991-3456	Debbie Stokes	2nd shift editor needed, Paltex trained, 5 years exp. See on Friday, 2:00 P.M. Address: 334 Congress Pkwy.

Figure 8.1: Sample Contact Sheet (Cont.)

	Type of Call	Company	Phone Number	Contact	Result/Next Step
5	Cold call	Silver Valley Comm. College	321-1111	Joe Presser, Manager, Media Resources	No openings, not interested. Send follow-up letter.
6	Referral from Joe Presser	Silver Valley CC	321-1111 (ext. 123)	Mike Demeter, Dept. Head, AV Comm. Dept.	Night video course possibility as instructor. Go see him next Mon. 3500 Comm. College Ave.
7	Cold call	Missouri Electric Cooperative	444-2000	Cathy Clark, Dir. of Public Relations	Not interested. Hung up on me!
8					
9					
10					

Television Production I (TVI) courses, the most basic production course for telecommunications majors.

At the time, Derrill was a professor in charge of a new area of study called Audio-Visual Technology at Cuyahoga (Cleveland) Community College. He hired part-time instructors to teach two television production courses that were part of the AVT degree. I got his name by calling the different campuses of the college, asking for the media centers, talking to the department heads (who had the authority to hire), asking about possible positions and eventually settling for referrals. (Always finish the conversation with, "Who else do you know who might need someone?") Derrill Dalby was one of the names that came up, and I called him.

He had had other inquiries from qualified people, had received many resumes and the television instructor positions were currently filled. But I persuaded him to see me.

I did this by saying that although the positions were filled, I would still like to meet with him and see his facility because I had heard about the program, was intrigued, and as a former instructor I wanted to see what he was teaching AVT students. He agreed to meet with me "for a few minutes."

As we talked, he indicated that he might be able to "give me a try" later in the year, but there were no openings right then, When I asked him if there was anyone else I should talk to, he referred me to the administration's media center. He even called on my behalf.

And that is why I urge you to meet with as many people as possible. You may have a pleasant voice, but nothing is as personal as being there in the flesh. And, as we have established, you *are* selling yourself. So, get an advantage over the others who call and mass-mail resumes. Meet with those contacts who are potential hiring sources.

My meeting with Derrill ultimately had a good ending. While he could not hire me at the time, his referral to the administration netted me a part-time job. And the following semester, he added a nighttime television production course that I started to teach (his other instructors would not teach at night). Three years later,

Derrill was hired by American Greetings to start an AV/TV department. I succeeded him as professor and department head.

LFAJ Axiom #5: Never Say the Word "Interview" to a Potential Employer

I might have never met with Derrill if I had said that I wanted to "set up an interview." Had I done so, he might have dismissed me by saying, "We really don't have anything, just send me your resume and we'll call you when we need you." Luckily, my emphasis was on meeting with him and seeing his facility.

The best search and placement executives in our industry have mastered the technique of never saying "interview." It is like that old game of whoever says "watermelon" first immediately loses. For employers, "interviewing someone" means you have to make a major decision and that is scary.

It's much better to say:

- "Let's *meet* on this . . ."
- "When can we *get together* to discuss this . . ."
- "Why don't we *talk about this* at your office . . ."
- "Let's *discuss* this . . ."
- "I think we should *work* on this over at your studio . . ."
- "I'd like to *drop by* and see your facility and perhaps talk to you . . ."

LFAJ Axiom #6: Do Not Overreact or Underreact to Your Present Employment Situation

If you should get laid off or come to the decision that it is time to leave, do not feel that your world is ending. It isn't. And your family needs you in the meantime, so do not go off the deep end.

Bob worked for a production house as a cameraman/editor. As work slackened, he was laid off. He decided to try freelancing, but for six months jobs were few and far between. Still, he learned to tighten his belt, live off his savings, and eventually one and then another client started to use him. Within two years, he had built up his clientele. He could have let his unemployment panic him, but he did not.

It's equally bad to be overeager. When you are looking for a job you might want to take the first one that comes your way. While that first job offer may be the immediate answer to your problems, take the time to look at it from all angles.

It may be that a few things need to be negotiated before you accept the offer. Or it may be that the offer is not what you really want and should be rejected.

But don't take too much time. Do not postpone the job hunt for another day.

Of course, you should do a self-appraisal to determine what you want to do, what is available and whether you should widen the search to consider other fields as well. It should take about a long weekend. Look at where you are and where you want to be and then define the steps you must take to reach your goal. You cannot become a producer overnight.

A person I know worked for a health organization for several years. One day, he was terminated due to cutbacks in the industry. He read a career book and decided to take "some time off and decide just what to do." Six months later, he still had not contacted one of the names I had given him as potential job sources. He said he was still "making sure what he wanted to do with his life."

Television, electronics and computers are quickly changing areas. If you are unemployed too long, your relative worth is greatly diminished. Evaluate your situation, do not rush into anything, but get back in the industry soon.

LFAJ Axiom #7: Be Honest

If they fired you, they fired you. The silver lining is that you learned from that experience. Even if your former employer is telling people that you are a rat, there is no need to lower yourself to his or her level.

Bob sent me a resume. He followed up with a personal call and visit, and I eventually hired him as a freelancer. Although he had had a bad ending with his previous employer, he handled the explanation professionally and smoothly. He told me that they had "some disagreements over some things that had been done," and he had decided to leave rather than create further animosity.

As mentioned in Chapter 5, a Robert Half employer survey estimated that 70% of all people in the United States have, at one time or another, been fired. For an employer to pass you up because you were fired would mean that the employer is limited to a very small segment of the total work population. Not necessarily a wise move.

As was emphasized in Chapter 7, be honest in your resumes and resume reels. Tell what you did and how you accomplished it. Explain the benefit of your past in terms of the employer's future. If you only ran camera on a show, say so. No one will fault you for not having certain experiences. It is far worse to say you have it and be found out later. At the very least, you will then be characterized as a liar. Anything you say from that point on will be viewed with suspicion.

LFAJ Axiom #8: Always Be Courteous, Always Send a Follow-up Letter or Note

While I have interviewed hundreds of people in my career thus far, I have received fewer than 10 thank-you letters or follow-up notes. Many job seekers mistakenly think that their task is over once the interview is finished. It is not.

Always send a letter thanking the interviewer for his or her time whether or not a job was available or an offer was extended.

A short note takes little time, and it will leave a positive impression that may come back to help you another day. It is important not to burn any bridges in your career, and it is equally important to build a few new ones from time to time. Consider a thank-you note as a little extra mortar.

LFAJ Axiom #9: Do Not Be Shy or Lazy, Sell Yourself

It will take a lot of work to get a new job. In many ways it is harder once you are in the industry. That is because the industry is close-knit, and people tend to know other organizations, how they work and the people within. You must take the initiative to change jobs. You cannot wait for someone to offer you a new job.

Conversely, you *can* wait to find the *right* job. It takes time, patience and skill. Learn to contact everyone and meet with as many people as possible. Networking is the name of the game. So is the art of learning to sell yourself.

Be prepared to answer all objections about why someone cannot see you. Do not send resumes if you can possibly avoid it. Like the British, keep a stiff upper lip and, like any sportsman, keep your eye on the ball, which is your goal of a new job.

LFAJ Axiom #10: Do Not Be a Job Hopper, Job Shopper or a Waste of People's Time

The question "When should I look for a new job?" is not easily answered. There is no exact time in anyone's career when he or she should start looking for a new job. A reasonable answer may well be, "Whenever you no longer are challenged by the position you are currently in." But because we are all different, challenges or the lack of them affect us at different times in our lives.

How often have you known someone who complains incessantly about a job only to be replaced eventually by someone who enjoys it and finds it to be exactly what he or she wanted in a career? Was the first person wrong to complain and feel stifled? Is the successor wearing rose-colored glasses? More than likely, the two simply have different "appetites" when it comes to what they demand out of a career.

HANDLING OBJECTIONS

When you are selling yourself, you will come across objections from potential employers. They will not want to see you even if they have an opening and a need to hire someone soon. There are many reasons and some of them are valid. But an even greater number are simply imagined.

What follows are some common objections you will run into and some ways you can handle them. These suggestions are best used if you practice them and make them a part of you. Only then will they sound natural and become an effective part of your search.

Remember, throughout this section, that what you are doing is qualifying the employer's objection in order to determine whether the objection is, in fact, real or imagined. You do not want to "burn any bridges" by being overly aggressive, but you do want to uncover the real situation and make yourself known without offending anyone.

It is a fine line, but the alternative is to simply accept that no one ever hires anyone and that the industry has all the people it is ever going to need. And that is simply not the case.

Objection: You Sound Good, But Send Me a Resume

In this situation you need to qualify the employer's need for a resume. It may actually be that company policy requires a resume before the interview. But then again, more than likely it is just a stalling tactic.

There are a number of ways to handle this objection:

- "Why?" (The answer will help you determine whether it is a real objection. However, continue to use one of the following questions to further define the objection.)
- "Obviously, I must have mentioned something in my background that interested you enough to want to see my resume. What specifically did you want to know about so that I can explain my experiences better for you?"
- "I have no problem with sending you my resume, but to be quite honest, I've had a large and diverse amount of experience. Rather than waste your time, what areas of my background are you specifically interested in that could help you and your company?"
- "As you know, in our industry, a written resume only tells part of the story. Why don't I meet with you and bring along a tape (portfolio, scripts, etc.) of my work so we can discuss exactly what I've done and how it can fit in with what you need?"
- "I'd be glad to send you my resume. Tell me, what specifically are you interested in so that I'll be sure to fully explain my relevant experiences."
- "I'm sure that in the past you've probably made a resume for yourself, so you can understand how a piece of paper doesn't really give the complete story of one's experiences. Why don't I come to your office? I'll bring the resume, you can review it and then I can help fill you in on all the areas where you need more information."
- "I'll personally deliver it to your studio. What time would be better for us to talk, 9:00 or 10:00 in the morning?"
- "To be perfectly honest with you, I'm still employed. Having my resume in other people's offices might look like I'm shopping around and really I'm just interested in what you do and may have to offer. I am interested in your company and would like to meet with you to

answer any questions you might have regarding my background. What day would be best for us to meet?"

- "There's no problem with sending you my resume, but really it only scratches the surface of my experience and what I am capable of doing for you. Why don't I bring it by and you could review it and then we could discuss my qualifications. Tell me, what would be a better time for me to come, Tuesday at 4:00 or Wednesday, first thing at 9:00?"

The last response utilizes what is known as the "alternate choice close." What you are doing is allowing the employer to make a decision with both possible answers being "yes." It is a powerful close and should become a part of your marketing approach. Closes, in general, allow the buyer (your potential employer) to make decisions, which, if handled correctly, will result in an interview and ultimately an offer.

Objection: We Are Not Hiring Anyone

This is often a knee-jerk response to anyone cold-calling for a job. What it means is that no one has said he or she is going to quit today. While that's fine, you did not call to take an employment survey. What you hope to accomplish, though, is to acquaint the contact with your credentials by understanding what the company does. This information will allow you to "tailor" what you say about your background to emphasize your fit with the company's needs.

Handle the objection quickly in order to get on with the business of meeting with the potential employer to talk about the business and your credentials. You will be surprised at how often "no opening" really means "we really could use someone like you, but hadn't thought of it."

There are several possible responses to this objection:

- "I'm not calling because I thought you'd have an opening, but rather to explain to you my unique qualifications. That way, should you have an opening in the future, you'll be able to remember me and what I can do for you."
- "I understand that you don't have any openings right now. Even if you did, I might not have the background for what you're looking for. But I do have diverse and extensive experience, and it may be that, sometime in the future, you may need someone with my background."
- "I understand you're not hiring, but I know you would want to be apprised of what I have to offer a facility like yours so that if anything happens *down the road* . . ."
- "I'm not sure I'd be right for a job with your company even if you had a position available. But if we could sit down for a few minutes and you could explain what you do, we might both come away knowing what we have to offer."
- "Even though you're not actively looking for someone, if I told you [fill in a FEATURE/ACCOMPLISHMENT/ BENEFIT of your own] . . . would that be enough to prompt you to talk with me and see what I can do?"
- "Is that just in your division, or company-wide?"
- "If you were hiring, what kind of background would you look for in a person?" [Then mention the parts of your background that fit what they are looking for.]
- "It doesn't surprise me that you have no openings. I didn't call to see if you did. I wanted you to be aware of the fact that I'm available and have [FAB] in my background. Now, when can we get together?"
- "I hear you saying that you don't have any openings on your staff. If I were to call the New York Giants, they'd probably say the same thing. But if I called them and told them I am a six-foot, 200-pound defensive lineman

who can run the 100-yard dash in 4.2 seconds and that I eat quarterbacks for breakfast, I think they'd want to see me. Don't you agree?" If the person on the other end says "no" then he or she is a little off center. If the answer is "yes" or "probably," then proceed with, "Well, that's the kind of player I am . . ."

- "I'm curious. Even though you may not have any openings right now, do you really feel you can pass up the opportunity to see what I've done and can do for you?"

Objection: You'll Have to Talk to Personnel

A few years ago, this was rarely used as an objection. With changes in the job market and mergers and acquisitions coming at a frantic pace, talking with the human resources department has to be judged on an individual basis. It may be that the personnel department may actually have to make the initial contact for paperwork and corporate protection policy. This is often true in large corporations. It is often best to work along with personnel rather than against them.

Still, sometimes having to talk to personnel is a smoke screen designed to put you off. You can determine the truthfulness of this objection with the following questions:

- "Does personnel hire people for you?"

If the answer is "yes," you need to determine how qualified they are to act on a call from you. Ask:

- "With television being such a specialized medium, how successful have they been in the past?"
- "Will they understand what you need and what I have done?"

If the answer is "no," then try to determine the function of the personnel department by asking:

- "What is their function in the hiring process?"
- "What is their function in relation to a specific position in the video department?" (Try to understand what role they play.)
- "What has been your past experience with personnel?"
- "How do they get qualified people from the video industry? Do they run ads? Where?"
- "Do they require resumes from prospective candidates? Do they use these resumes to screen people in . . . or out? Does the video department get to see ALL of the resumes pertaining to people with television or communications backgrounds?"

By asking questions you will be able to see the relationships between the two departments and you can then plan to work with them, if you choose to.

CONCLUSION

Looking for a new job takes time, effort and money. Start with people you know and begin a list of contacts. Follow through on everyone and expect to receive plenty of objections. Practice your phone speech to possible employers.

Practice how you will explain your background to potential employers using FEATURE-ACCOMPLISHMENT-BENEFIT presentations. And practice how you will handle various objections.

Do not be lazy or shy in your job search because looking for a new job is clearly up to you. Set your goals and think about each necessary step needed to advance toward them.

There are no set rules about when you should and should not look for a new position. The decision should be guided by what you expect to achieve in your career and your career goals. Be persistent, but not obnoxious in your search. Acknowledge the contributions others have made to your career. Someday you may be contributing to others' career searches.

Look first at the organization you are currently working for. If there is no advancement possible, then begin the difficult but rewarding task of looking for a new job. When you have made the decision to change jobs, never take the counteroffer. It is your life and your career. It is up to you to look for a new job. No one can do it for you.

If you have not made solid career plans, Chapter 9 examines the many career paths available in nonbroadcast television.

9
Career Paths in Nonbroadcast Video

In this chapter we will cover some of the different directions your career can take in nonbroadcast video. We will describe the major job categories within the industry and explore the qualifications needed to move up and beyond your current position. We will also explore where nonbroadcast video fits into the overall corporate and educational spectrums. This way, you will be able to see where you should look.

Although the descriptions are general, the positions are standard throughout the industry. An editor in Maine is the same as an editor in Los Angeles. The equipment may vary, but the employee's capabilities do not.

Also, it is not uncommon for people in this industry to be "hyphenates," that is, people whose responsibilities overlap more than one category as a result of multiple talents or the nature of nonbroadcast video, which often requires a person to wear many hats. Therefore, one might be a producer-director or cameraperson-editor.

After each job description is a section entitled *Next Step*, which indicates available career paths, based on a successful tenure in that position. The intent is to show the paths most widely traveled and therefore the most common rungs on the career ladder. A cameraperson may develop into a director or editor, but rarely makes the jump to executive producer or department manager. Exceptions, of course, do occur.

The *Next Step* is not intended to suggest that there need be a next step for you from any of these positions. Rather, it is merely a signpost to guide you. It is also not intended to suggest that these are the only career paths that can be taken. You may decide to leave the nonbroadcast video industry. If that is your intention, moving out of nonbroadcast video is discussed in Chapter 10.

PRODUCTION JOB DESCRIPTIONS

Production or Technical Assistant

This is often the first rung on the career ladder. Everything that is mundane or tedious in nonbroadcast television is the responsibility of production and technical assistants because these are starting positions. Duties range from going for coffee during a production to cleaning up after one. It may also involve taking notes during a pre-production meeting, building sets, setting up the studio, gathering sets and props, setting lights, carrying equipment on remote shoots, setting up microphones, duplicating tapes, acting as the "continuity person" on shoots and basically assisting anyone and everyone connected with a video production. When someone has to go for something, the production assistant is the one.

The production assistant has an important function. Good production assistants, who take their jobs seriously and strive to learn and contribute, are worth their weight in gold. They have a zest for their jobs and enhance their worth by being in on everything. They can be the glue that holds the entire production department together. With a desire to see a job through to the end and the unique gift of thoroughness, they can save the department much time and effort.

The intensity you show in your first job can determine the length of your stay in the nonbroadcast video industry.

Often, the best video department managers turn themselves back into glorified production assistants. Because of their managerial duties, they realize that they cannot keep up with quickly changing technology in order to be useful as an editor or cameraperson. But they can contribute their organizational skills by keeping the individual productions on target, so they often act as production assistants during productions. Entry-level people should understand the necessity of this position and the need for things to be done right.

Production assistants work a minimum of 40 hours a week. The position requires basic clerical and production skills and allows the employee to learn a variety of things. The day often begins with opening up the facility and preparing lights, sets, tapes and anything else that is needed for the day's productions. Production assistants attend production meetings and are assigned responsibilities in the productions.

In smaller facilities assistants will have a number of jobs assigned to them, depending upon their capabilities. Production assistants may do everything from operating a camera to running a teleprompter during a studio production. Often, assistants will hook up recording and playback equipment in both the studio and field. With enough experience, production assistants may perform simple edits and put together a work print or rough edit.

On remote productions, production assistants will help carry equipment to the site and be responsible for some of the setup. During the shoot, they may hold prompter copy, assist in crowd control (a camera is often greeted with lots of interest by the public), operate a light deflector or handle a shotgun microphone.

Salary Range

Starting at minimum wage, production assistants' salaries generally range from $10,000 to $15,000 per year.

Prerequisites

Although 10 years ago this position required little more than a desire to work in video, the number of graduating communications majors has pushed the prerequisite to a two-year associate or four-year communications degree. Prior experience makes a difference in the level of opportunity the position affords. Good production and clerical skills as well as technical expertise are necessary.

Prospects of Employment

Due to fairly high turnover in the position, production assistants enjoy good prospects for employment. Furthermore, depending on how quickly they learn and adapt, they are in an excellent position for advancement. In nonbroadcast television, you will find higher level production and supervisory people who started with the same organization as production assistants. Nonbroadcast video departments often promote their own assistants first rather than hire from the outside.

Next Step

The lower you are on the career ladder the more steps are available to you. An assistant's job allows you to decide what segments of nonbroadcast video appeal to you. A typical next step might be assistant editor, technician, assistant director, technical director, assistant producer, junior writer, cameraperson, remote technician or remote location assistant. As with all positions, remember that Rome was not built in a day; your career is similar. With patience, hard work and experience, the sky is the limit.

Videographer

The videographer or cameraperson is responsible for camera selection, setup and shot composition. (See Figure 9.1.) Good videographers also know a great deal about how cameras work. They usually have one or two favorite cameras that they personally admire and like to work with. Good videographers know lighting,

Figure 9.1: Cameraperson, Joan Dollard, readies her camera
to film the training segment of a news program.

both for the studio and the field, and can tell the producer
what equipment might be needed by evaluating the script and the
studio or location. They also help the director with visualization
of the script and make suggestions accordingly.

Entry-level freelancers often start as videographers. However,
good freelance videographers can make a living doing this and
nothing more, particularly if they are located around urban
centers. Once they achieve a certain reputation, they can live anywhere. A good "eye," that is, someone with a good sense of composition, will always be in demand.

Videographers are responsible for handling camera and shot
selection, lighting setup and composition of the shot and are
responsible for getting the program committed correctly on tape.
They may produce and edit smaller format video and may act as
producer on smaller productions.

The work environment is usually split between studio and
remote locations. Because nonbroadcast video has evolved to a
point where remote location shooting is done more often than
studio shooting (estimates range from 60% to 80%), the ability to

carry the equipment to the location has become an important consideration. While cameras and VCRs have shrunk in size, lights, tripods, blank tapes, audio equipment and other necessities have pushed the typical weight of a single camera EFP (electronic field production) to between 300 and 400 pounds. This job is not for weaklings!

The nature of the work often requires long and sometimes difficult hours. I have worked with videographers at 4:00 A.M. just to prepare for a shoot. Overtime is often the norm rather than the exception. I've had crews work 16 hours straight.

Salary Range

Salaries range from $15,000 to $25,000 per year. Freelance videographers in major markets can make as much as $35,000 to $40,000 per year. As with all freelance positions, the cost of being in business for oneself must be taken into consideration.

Prerequisites

An undergraduate degree in television, photography or film is necessary. Two to four years of production experience is usually required, and it helps if you show particular expertise in visual layout.

Videographers take direction well and know how to work with a variety of people. This is one production position that requires constant practice. There are many who call themselves videographers, but few who are really successful enough to develop their own style. Style is very important in this position. Directors rely heavily on the videographer's ability to "see" and visually interpret the production. Therefore, a prerequisite is spending a lot of time shooting and having your work critiqued.

A good understanding of light and lighting instruments is a necessity. This is where still photography experience is important.

Videographers who understand the overall production process, especially editing, have an advantage. Because they know what an editor needs to create a program, they know what to shoot to enable the editor to do the job properly. A videographer's axiom is "If the shot isn't there, it can't be edited into the program." Great videographers understand this and go to great lengths to shoot everything an editor might need to produce a quality program.

Prospects of Employment

The prospects for continued employment are good. Because the actual layout of a shot allows for personal interpretation, capable videographers have little trouble keeping busy. There are levels of expertise in camera work. Many videographers are capable technicians who can do a workmanlike job. The few who develop a unique style and continually look for a creative angle or lighting treatment are usually well-known and much used.

With the proliferation of nonbroadcast video programming, the need for videographers has expanded greatly. Videographers' ranks are growing, and so is the demand for their services.

Next Step

From here on, all positions can be career positions that represent an end in themselves. It is not unusual for someone to remain a videographer all his or her professional life. But videographers who aspire to something different do have a few select avenues open to them.

Generally, all production positions are available to videographers. Editors, lighting directors and audio engineers, for example, require technical experience that videographers pick up through their work.

Moving to a director's position requires more than technical expertise. The abilities to see the overall picture of a production and to work with and motivate a variety of people in different situations require good organizational skills. A director is often, in reality, a part-time manager of a group of people for a short period of time. If your desire is to be a director, then development of these skills is required to insure your success.

Editor

This person, at the very least, operates the editing equipment. Sometimes, editors work under the direction of a producer or director and assist by not just editing but by making suggestions as to how a program should be cut. They may have full responsibility for taking the raw footage and putting together the entire program based on a script. They can operate cuts-only type equipment or multiple input computerized equipment that includes digital effects, character generation, graphic systems and audio mixing and sweetening equipment.

Editors either work with a producer or director or, as is often the case in smaller settings, may act on their own. They are responsible for selecting the best "takes" for a production and deciding on the transitions from shot to shot. The quality of the video and audio on the edited master is the editor's responsibility.

The work environment in which editors operate is usually entirely within the confines of an editing bay. Editing bays range from simple to complex. Due to the nature of their work, editors must relish challenge, long hours and be able to meet deadlines.

It is the rare producer who is not up against a deadline; therefore, editors must learn to work with too little time to complete too large a project. And the really good editors are the ones who pull off this magic act time and again and please their clients by doing so. This type of editor is used constantly, enjoys a high degree of client loyalty and is never out of work.

Most producers agree that skilled editors with a creative flair are worth their weight in gold. As the creative process heats up in the editing suite, clients and producers will often go only to certain facilities so they can work with their favorite editors who have a genuine creative spirit and an ability to keep deadlines.

There are not as many freelance editors as there are freelance videographers. This is due, in part, to the inaccessibility of editing equipment for potential editors to practice on.

Salary Range

Salaries range from $18,000 to $35,000 per year. The large range is a result of the specialized skills that a particular editor has with specific types and models of equipment. Editing suites are custom-made and often have different types of equipment, therefore, an editor's compensation is based on his or her expertise with the particular equipment. Salaries may be also based on the editor's knowledge of the organization and ability to get along with various clients.

Prerequisites

Although a four-year degree in communications, public relations, advertising or motion picture photography is not mandatory, the bulk of editors seem to have degrees. Certainly, course work enabling one to understand the creative process of putting together a production will help ensure success as an editor. In fact, in the production course I have taught over the years, the students who seem to understand the editing process best are often the most successful in the industry.

The increasing sophistication of editing equipment requires hands-on experience. This experience can be acquired while employed in other production positions where editing bays are used. Interns, production assistants, videographers and even directors can gain vital experience by making time to learn the equipment. Obviously, an understanding of computers is also a necessity for this position.

Some of the larger equipment manufacturers, like CMX and Paltex, offer courses to teach editors the capabilities of specific models. Editors who have taken such courses will have an advantage when looking for a job.

Prospects of Employment

Employment prospects are very good. There are too few good editors to go around. Editing often represents the bottleneck in the production stream of work. Good editors who know their equipment's capabilities and who have a personality fit to work with different people have almost no problem in finding continuous employment. Even those who are more technical than people-oriented find the marketplace open and inviting. With editing equipment changing as fast as software can be adapted, editors are very much in demand.

Next Step

Editors in nonbroadcast video often double as directors and, in smaller production facilities, producers. The flexibility of the nonbroadcast video industry often allows one person to operate in a number of positions. Therefore, a logical move for an editor might be either to the producer's or director's chair.

Editors along with directors are not considered management, but are production area employees.

Writer

Writers are actually translators who evaluate the clients' needs and transfer them to video. Writers take an idea, research the source material and develop scripts that visualize the program. They are able to take a concept and commit it to paper. Successful writers must be creative and able to analyze something they may know very little about. Often, their job on a particular project is completed before anyone else's is. Once the script is accepted they generally move on to the next project. Sometimes, they may be called back to rewrite, particularly if many changes are needed.

Writers evaluate what the need for the proposed production is and then, like interpreters, design scripts to meet those needs. They take the program's concept and distill it into words and actions. Nonbroadcast video writers are usually flexible enough to write for print, technical publications, promotional pieces, multi-image slide programs and audio-only productions as well.

Writers are responsible for the research on the proposed program and frequently spend time reading about the topic and interviewing experts. Sometimes writers are responsible for the program's concept and often bring script outlines for approval by the client or producer. Once approved, they write the actual shooting script for the production.

Writers may also be involved in interpreting and evaluating the finished program. The writer's perspective must always deal with the question: "Did the program meet its objectives?"

Salary Range

Writers can expect to earn $18,000 to $40,000 per year. Assignments often overlap into other fields, such as advertising, speech writing and technical (manual) writing. Freelancers and part-timers also use their skills as writers for the nonbroadcast television field.

Prerequisites

Writers' backgrounds are often based in print, English or literary fields. Many have acquired four-year and advanced academic degrees, usually in English, writing, communications, advertising or theater. Unlike most other positions where video was a primary goal, nonbroadcast television writers may have begun their careers in a field other than video and later changed course when they discovered the challenges and their own unique talents.

Educators will tell you that it is hard to teach the skill of writing. It is harder yet to teach the skills of scriptwriting. Good writers for print do not always successfully make the switch to writing for video. That is because good scriptwriting deviates from some of the axioms of good prose. Successful scriptwriters will find on-the-job training and practice to be a necessity.

The glamour of pounding the Underwood typewriter has largely been displaced by the word processor. Therefore, an understanding of computers is essential.

Prospects of Employment

The outlook for employment is very good as video production needs are expanding. The many writers I know have little time to do all the offered projects and may have to refuse some or delegate them to other writers.

As with videographers, freelance opportunities abound. Writers who work for production houses and corporations often expand their horizons by taking on outside projects. Some eventually move to freelancing where they can ply their craft for others. Because most writers enjoy a high degree of satisfaction with their positions, the need for advancement through promotion does not seem very evident. Also, the writer has the advantage of not having to march to the changing technological beat of video and learn new equipment and capabilities.

Next Step

Writers' talents are unique. Although associated with the production process, their work actually precedes production. While their skills are transferable to other forms of writing, their background tends not to lead directly to other production positions.

The writer who seeks advancement will often find opportunities outside of video in public relations, advertising, print and internal business communications. Those staying within the video field will have to either develop the technical expertise to assist in productions or the managerial skills necessary to take on the responsibilities of a director.

Audiovisual Specialist

AV or media specialists analyze the production requests and determine the medium best suited to reaching the goal. Not confined to using only television, media specialists have experience in various media, including slide-tape presentations, audiocassette productions, graphics and photography. AV specialists set up the media programs and troubleshoot equipment problems.

The work environment is usually cramped with the media specialists' equipment. They often find it necessary to work long hours due to the fact that they are usually the only one in the department.

Salary Range

Media specialists can expect to earn from $16,000 to $28,000 per year.

Prerequisites

A two-year audiovisual associate's degree or a four-year B.S. in communications is necessary. In educational settings, some states require certification for audiovisual specialists. Two to three years of working with a variety of media are necessary to obtain a broad background.

Prospects of Employment

Employment prospects are good. Media centers, in general, are growing. Also, corporations and nonprofit institutions, realizing the need for various media, are adding AV specialists to their staffs to perform a variety of functions.

Next Step

The career path of the AV specialist has two distinct possible directions. One is based on the continued growth of a small department into providing more in-depth services and thereby providing the opportunity for the specialist to move into a supervisory role. The other option involves the exploration and development of a distinct production talent, such as videographer.

Graphic Designer

Graphic designers must understand the technology of character generators and paint boxes as well as the goals and needs of the program. They are usually instrumental in set design and execution. They are responsible for all the graphics and visuals used within a production.

Graphic designers in smaller facilities may wear several hats and provide graphics and layout for flyers, newsletters, brochures, manuals and technical drawings. Desktop publishing can also be a large responsibility for the graphic designer.

Salary Range

Graphic designers earn from $15,000 to $25,000 per year.

Prerequisites

A degree in art or graphics is preferable. A degree with experience in communications, video and computers is helpful.

Two to three years of experience in different artistic media help the intern or production assistant to make the transition to graphic designer. Computer graphics are such an integral part of nonbroadcast video productions that the more experience one can get on character generators or computer palettes, the better. Even though various equipment models do different things, graphic designers can learn the programs quickly. Desktop publishing can give artists experience in electronic layout and design.

Prospects of Employment

Employment prospects are very good. Interns and production assistants who take the time and have the inclination to teach themselves the equipment are usually prime candidates to move into this position.

Next Step

Because of their artistic training, the career paths of graphic designers are specialized. Like writers, they may find advancement in fields other than video. Often, their close working relationships with directors and editors enable them to move into other positions in nonbroadcast television. Graphic designers with a photographic leaning can become videographers.

Technician

Technicians operate all types of the most common video and audio equipment. They serve as the technical members of the crew and do minor maintenance and troubleshooting of the equipment. Any major repairs would probably be sent out. Technicians usually set up studios, VCRs and monitors in training facilities and assist in productions. They are generally a step or two above the production assistant position. They must understand the technical make-up of the equipment and perform routine setup and calibration functions. In smaller facilities, they serve as a kind of quasi-engineer by making certain AV and video equipment are performing up to specifications.

The technician's environment is often in the AV or video area. Quite often, they do not have an office and usually like the freedom and variety of the position. Similar to the production assistant, they are often jacks-of-all-trades while not mastering any.

Salary Range

Technicians' salaries range from $17,000 to $26,000 per year.

Prerequisites

Technicians must have a minimum two-year associate's degree in electronics or audiovisual technology. They often have at least two to five years production experience and generally display an interest in equipment.

Next Step

In small departments, technicians are often in line to become department heads or supervisors. Some, who are interested in equipment, take additional courses or gain experience to become engineers. Others enjoy production and may move into editors' or videographers' positions.

Engineer

Engineers are responsible for the technical quality of all video and related audio equipment. They insure that the systems are running according to technical standards and operate all the test equipment necessary to calibrate and time the sophisticated television equipment.

Engineers do preventive maintenance on the equipment and are usually capable of rebuilding equipment and doing major repairs, such as video head replacement, chip diagnosis and replacement, and rewiring of components. Usually they train others in the proper operation and simple correction of video equipment. For example, an engineer would show videographers how to align a camera so that they could do it properly in the field.

Engineers evaluate and recommend television and related support equipment, design the installation, and then supervise the placement and wiring. They love the technical end of video and are constantly updating themselves. For example, if you have a question about high-definition television (HDTV), the engineer would be the right person to ask. It has probably been in the trade journals for months, and he or she has read up on it.

The engineer's desk is often a workbench strewn with repair and maintenance projects. The engineers I've known are usually quiet, but have definite convictions about equipment. For example, I've known some who prefer Sony equipment, and others who would not touch Sony for any reason.

Engineers work wherever there is video and AV equipment. More often they can be found under or behind the equipment than in front of it. They can make immediate sense of technical journals and schematics and look at video from a purely technical standpoint.

Engineers are a necessary component of today's nonbroadcast television facility. Where it was once possible to hook up equipment without constant engineering support, as nonbroadcast video proliferates and grows, so do the systems and the needs for quality engineering support.

Engineers are needed to keep the highly sophisticated electronic equipment operating correctly. They are, perhaps, the employees most in demand in nonbroadcast video because of a great shortage of qualified people. That is partially because there is no formal schooling for engineers. Schools rarely train television technicians and, besides, the equipment is changing so quickly that it would be difficult for a formal course to keep up with the changes.

Most engineers have been sent to the various engineering courses offered by manufacturers. Sony, Panasonic, Hitachi, Grass Valley and Microtime provide such instruction.

Salary Range

Engineers' salaries range from $26,000 to $39,000 per year.

Prerequisites

Engineers hold a four-year degree in either engineering or electronics or a specialized degree from an electronics institution. They also have three to five years practical experience as an engineer's assistant or service technician.

Prospects of Employment

The prospects for engineers are excellent. If the engineer has production capabilities and can double as a production assistant, videographer or editor, the employment outlook is even better. There are not enough engineers to fill the needs of all the facilities that have increasingly complex systems and little engineering support.

If the nonbroadcast video department does not have a video engineer, most engineering and maintenance support comes from the local equipment vendor. Similar to an automobile dealership, most vendors make money on *selling* equipment, not *repairing* or *maintaining* it. Therefore, the engineering department is frequently not the vendor's top priority.

This problem has been solved, to some degree, by independent television engineering companies that can service several departments that might not be able to afford or need the services of a full-time engineer.

However, as illustrated in Chapter 2, the nonbroadcast video market is growing and is expected to continue to grow. In addition, the equipment is becoming increasingly sophisticated. Engineers, particularly those who can assist in production, are necessary to keep up with this growth.

Any engineer with some production experience will find that nonbroadcast video is a fertile area for job hunting. Why? First, there are not enough engineers to fill the available positions. Second, the type of logical thinking that engineering requires seems to run contrary to the creative process used in production. An engineer with skills in both areas is a valuable commodity.

Next Step

Engineers looking for advancement can work for video equipment vendors. Within the organization, engineers can pick up production skills that will enable them to do more; this also increases their marketability in other production centers. The reason for this is that most nonbroadcast video centers are staffed with people who wear several hats. An engineer-director or an engineer-editor is very valuable to a broader range of departments and facilities.

Even without production experience, the engineer can grow by becoming knowledgeable about a variety of equipment. He can then go on to larger facilities, such as production houses, and he can even leave the nonbroadcast television field, as explained in Chapter 10, to enter the broadcast field as an engineer.

MANAGEMENT JOB DESCRIPTIONS

Director, producer, executive producer, supervisor, department manager and sales executive are positions that require business skills as well as production experience. Necessary business skills include accounting, business communications, management skills, leadership abilities, data processing experience and the ability to communicate ideas. Business education and experience, however gained, is necessary for any production person seeking a move into management. The following positions all require identifiable management skills as a background prerequisite.

Director

The director is the field marshal of the production. He directs the actual production either in the field or in the studio. He is in charge of selecting and directing the talent, placement of stages, sets and props, the type and style of lighting, placement and movement of cameras and shots, the movement of the talent and any other decisions in relation to the actual production.

He works with the producer to insure that deadlines and budgets are being met and often works with the editor to post-produce the program.

To be a successful director, one must be able to make decisions on a number of production factors and work with a variety of people while keeping the goals and objectives of the production in mind.

A number of freelance directors assume more than just directorial duties. They are often given some of the producer's responsibilities and, when called upon to edit a program, may act as a liaison between the client or producer and the editor.

Organizational and managerial skills are an absolute necessity to be an effective director. Quick decision-making abilities and an understanding of how to conduct negotiations with clients or production personnel are also needed, as are diplomacy and the ability to agree while making a point.

The director's work environment is wherever the shoot is taking place. It can be in the studio with a large crew or it can be outside in any number of locations throughout the world with crews as small as just one other person—a videographer. This is not to say that remote locations have smaller concerns for the director.

For example, the awards presentation staged in Hawaii that was mentioned in Chapter 1 required two tons of equipment, a crew of 10, months of preparation and considerable attention to detail.

Salary Range

Directors earn from $22,000 to $35,000 per year.

Prerequisites

Directors are considered to be management employees. Therefore, a four-year degree in television with managerial experience is necessary. A minimum of five years production experience is also required.

Prospects of Employment

The employment outlook is good. Directors, like videographers, develop their own styles and reputations. They tend to specialize and, because of their familiarity with the turf, they know how to get things done efficiently, who to use, where to go to get things done and keep their mark stamped on the production. This is a position that freelancers are starting to move into. Certain directors are becoming known for specialities, such as "live" programs, industrial training programs and employee communications programs. As this occurs, job prospects are increasing.

Next Step

Because the tasks of the producer are often carried out by a qualified director, there is movement between the two positions. Directors who want more control over their productions often become producers.

The opposite is also true. Producers who tire of the vast amount of responsibility and decision making and want to get back to the production side of video often go back to being a director.

Directors often become "hyphenates." Director-editor and producer-director are two of the most common.

Directors who opt to stay in the production arena, but want to add more to their experience can take on either editor or writer responsibilities. Both require on-the-job training. Rarely are both added, perhaps because of their diversity in skills or the lack of time.

Directors with good managerial skills can make the jump into upper management. But a word of caution—after being a director, all other jobs will take you away from production. When you stop being a full-time director, you are leaving the producing of programs.

Producer

Nonbroadcast television, as differentiated from broadcast television or the cinema, often requires producers to lead double lives by requiring them to be the manager of the video department as well as a producer. They work with clients to determine their needs and to suggest a course of action.

Producers usually analyze the target audience and the program's objective in order to determine whether the program will, in effect, hit the mark. They work with the client to decide on budget and script direction. In nonbroadcast video, they may elect to write the script themselves if they have that skill. Similarly, depending on the size of the production, they may either select a director or direct the project themselves.

Producers are responsible for all aspects above and below the line of the production: on budget and on time are two areas of their concern. They are responsible for the overall direction of the project and may have other corollary interests, such as promotion or accompanying written materials.

Producers must see that the props and sets are ordered and assembled and approve the talent selected by the director. They coordinate the activities of the writer, director, production personnel, editor and talent. They are responsible for bringing the program in on time, within the projected budget and designed to meet the user's needs and stated objectives.

They are also responsible, after the production is completed, for assisting in determining the program's effectiveness.

Because of the nature of the position, producers spend only part of their time on the actual production. Most of their time is spent managing, determining logistics, working with numbers, meeting with clients, gathering the technical information needed to design the program and designing tests to evaluate the results.

Large corporations may have several producers on staff. Similarly, as the independent freelance market grows, producers have been striking out on their own and enjoying success. In nonbroadcast television, two or three major clients may be all an independent producer can handle.

Staff producers enjoy a respected position within their organization. Ranking with other business specialists, producers are usually well regarded as consultants and treated as experts.

Most producers pay for this respect with an overzealous approach to the business that can translate into many hours and much work. The best producers seem to have all the work they could possibly handle and still find time to take on more.

Salary Range

Producers earn from $25,000 to $36,000 per year.

Prerequisites

Producers must have a B.S. in communications or a related field; sometimes advanced degrees are required as well. Business courses and managerial experience figure heavily in their background. This is not a position for someone with poor people skills. Ten or more years of production and management experience are required.

Prospects of Employment

The employment outlook is good. As you travel up the non-broadcast video career ladder, specialization can be both a necessity and a hindrance. As with any higher level position, greater windows of opportunity open, but the employee spends longer periods of time in one position. You will find interesting positions open at this level, but you might also find yourself overqualified for some.

Next Step

The producer position within most organizations is actually a department-head function. Thus, the next step may entail meeting the needs of the organization in other ways. There are a number of management tracks available to the producer.

Producers, who specialize in designing programs to meet specific needs, have found themselves writing speeches, designing internal and external news releases and designing live action or multi-image programs. If communications departments are assigned to the producer–department head, he or she may become a department director, manager or supervisor.

As pointed out earlier, some of the career paths for producers will lead out of nonbroadcast video. (See Chapter 10.)

Supervisor

There are often many layers of management. The supervisor position is often the first step into actual line management and is, therefore, the lowest rung on the administrative career ladder.

Supervisors work with clients and may work with a variety of audiovisual media. They may be responsible for an entire media department or simply a section of one. They are responsible for the scheduling of media resources and act as producers in the sense that they work to get the overall program completed.

Supervisors generally give input on budgets, salaries and hiring, but rarely have final say in such matters. They may work with facilities and people inside the organization or they may have to schedule productions outside. While they may develop departmental goals and objectives, they are more likely to administer decrees from a higher authority rather than set policy themselves.

Supervisors do not necessarily have a video production background. Some large companies pride themselves on promoting supervisors from other areas. Such policy keeps a distance between the supervisor and his or her area and, the logic goes, the supervisor and the organization are better for it. Supervisors, therefore, are often employees who are being groomed for ascension up the corporate and organizational ladder.

Salary Range

Supervisors earn from $27,000 to $38,000 per year.

Prerequisites

A supervisor needs a minimum of a four-year degree; postgraduate work is often a plus. Again, it is not necessary for a media supervisor to have a television or media background. However, those who are from the nonbroadcast video arena must display supervisory capabilities in order to be considered for advancement to this position.

Prospects of Employment

The employment outlook is very good. This is a position that tends to have a significant amount of turnover because it is considered a first step in administration. Actually moving into this position may be harder than excelling at it. Media people often forget the overall goals of the organization and tend to adopt the viewpoints of their fellow production types. As a supervisor, you must be able to carry out the commands and plans of the people above you. This management position requires solid people, organizational and leadership skills. Good leaders will find the prospect of employment very good and advancement even better.

Next Step

Manager or media department director is often the next step for a supervisor. Increased responsibilities are earned, often accompanied by a rigid set of standards. Supervisors who prove their abilities are often rewarded with increases in power, compensation and title.

Manager or Media Department Director

Managers or media department directors are responsible for all aspects of the audiovisual media department. They are responsible for short-term and long-range planning, budgeting, day-to-day operations, staff hiring and firing, developing of policies and procedures for the department, and overall direction of the department. They may work with clients and thereby function as ad hoc executive producers. Often the day-to-day interfacing with clients is left to producers under their command.

Managers are responsible for all schedule coordination and working with users to maximize usage of the media department. They are responsible for all operating budgets and capital expenditures. They determine what pieces of equipment are purchased and which formats will be used. It is their duty to plan for all new technology and to continue to support existing systems. For example, the study, marketing and eventual implementation of a satellite network for a corporation or institution would be the complete responsibility of the manager. That program's success or failure is also the manager's responsibility and would reflect directly on the manager's career.

Probably, the most understated, yet critical, function of managers is the ongoing marketing and promotion of the department's services. In today's fluctuating business atmosphere, it is more important than ever before that the services and products of media services divisions be marketed again and again to potential clients. New uses for production services and new products, like interactive or satellite programs, must be developed and explained to potential media department users.

An example of this type of marketing is illustrated by the change in status of the employee news program. The 1986 Brush Report showed the increased popularity of employee news programs.[1] Alert nonbroadcast video managers noticed this trend and many were able to successfully market employee news programs to their clients. It is evident, then, that successful managers are often the ones who are successful at marketing their ideas.

Salary Range

Media department directors earn from $32,000 to $50,000+ per year.

Prerequisites

A four-year degree in business, marketing, communications or any other related area is considered a bare minimum for this

---

[1] Judith M. and Douglas P. Brush, *Private Television Communications: The New Directions* (Cold Spring, NY: HI Press, 1986), pp. 64–65.

position. Advanced degrees are increasingly becoming the norm. Experience of five to ten plus years is necessary. Experience dealing with people, budgets and the organization is required before advancement into this position.

Prospects of Employment

The employment outlook is very good. As departments continue to grow, so do the needs for effective managers. Good marketing skills guarantee the individual manager continued success.

Next Step

Promotions include the addition of other responsibilities. Beyond video, these areas include training, audiovisual, print, graphics, photography, data processing, advertising, trade shows and public relations. A career path taking this route would likely extend to the position of director of corporate communications—a position some former nonbroadcast media department directors or managers now occupy.

Unfortunately, there is not a market for freelance managers. However, because of the skills necessary to be successful, some managers opt to become freelance consultants. Media consultants cover a multitude of areas with their services and are as diverse as can be. There are consultants who dispense advice on production, productivity, media selection, equipment and facilities selection and design, satellite network organization, scriptwriting and program design.

It would be safe to say that if climbing the corporate ladder is not your idea of long-term growth, then a consultancy may be the way for you to use your skills and be your own boss.

SUPPORT STAFF

Every nonbroadcast video department has support staff people who may eventually move into the production area. Secretaries, bookkeepers, tape librarians, word processors, clerks and receptionists are just a few support positions that help make video departments work. They are often as important and critical to the department's overall performance as the production staff. Sometimes they are even more important.

While some entry-level people have taken these support staff positions with the idea of moving into the production area, many stay in the positions because they prefer the challenge and freedom of the jobs. A good support staff makes the department run well, can alert management to any problems, and is often the glue that keeps the department together.

Salary Range

Salaries for entry-level administrative positions range from $12,000 to $25,000 per year. While advancement is always possible, many employees prefer to remain in "niche-type" positions that require unique skills. Such staff is often well-organized, highly motivated, and detail-oriented. Secretarial school graduation is often a bare minimum; college degrees in communications, journalism, business management and accounting are becoming more prevalent.

Makeup Artists

Makeup artists are often freelancers in nonbroadcast television. Their experience is usually based in fashion and other print photography. Video may be only a part of their overall client base.

Talents

Talents are also freelancers in nonbroadcast video. While the industry is likely to use amateurs in these positions, professional talents help make high-quality productions. Most professional talents are members of the American Federation of Television and Radio Announcers and, therefore, their compensation is regulated by the professional association.

Amateurs, such as department heads of companies or even video department personnel are often used in nonbroadcast television, particularly in organizations that must keep a close watch on the bottom line of each production. Though not as easy to work with or of the quality of professionals, amateurs do add an element of reality to the productions. Many corporate departments use their own people to augment professional talents. Or they may elect to use their own people because the audience likes to see co-workers on television. In addition, the high-profile responsibility of appearing in a production is looked upon as a benefit to the individual.

ALLY YOURSELF WITH THE BOTTOM LINE

Each year, *Broadcasting* magazine surveys its readers to determine career paths. Generally speaking, all broadcast personnel are broken into three main categories: engineering, sales and production. And of these three main areas, which one would you guess provides over 80% of all station managers each and every year?

If you answered sales, you are correct. Approximately 10% come from production, and even fewer from engineering. The reason is obvious. In our free enterprise system, those who are closest to the profit line are perceived as being more in touch with the organization's needs and are promoted accordingly. It is felt that because of their sales experiences, they are better equipped to handle the pressures of upper management.

While you can argue this hypothesis for an eternity, the bottom line is that if you intend to climb the managerial career ladder in your organization, you should tie yourself closely to the profit-making part of the business.

Nathan Sanbul, former head of Merrill Lynch's video department and now a consultant to the industry, has explained in seminars for managers of corporate television departments at the ITVA national convention that departments fail when they have little or no relation to the company's bottom line. Of course, the same is true for the individual in the nonbroadcast video field. Gene Kutina, Director of Communications for Cigna Insurance, explained, "If you're going to survive in a nonbroadcast environment, you had better be able to show a direct connection to the organization's bottom line."

This means that experience in producing training tapes for the sales department is a positive factor in your background, as is making communications tapes designed for your organization's outside customers. In fact, anything you can do that brings you closer to what your organization does will enhance your experience, make you more valuable and increase your chances of promotion.

WHAT IF YOUR GOAL IS NOT MANAGEMENT?

In America, great emphasis is placed on getting ahead. Often, people perceive this as eventually becoming the boss. But getting ahead does not necessarily mean that you should strive to become the boss, or that there is something wrong with you if you don't want to be the boss.

In colleges today, great emphasis is being put on management skills. That's fine, but, especially in video, it takes many people to put together a department, but only one manager to lead it. And while there is a lack of good managers, there are many managers who would rather not be in the position they are in. They were happy as editors, directors, or writers, but now they are unhappy as managers. Many employees enjoy what they do, desire to advance in their career, but do not want to ascend into a position that requires the management of people, time and resources. They like being editors, directors or writers.

In nonbroadcast video, you do not need to be the boss to be successful. Virtually every position can breed continual success for you through the medium's need for creativity and for each part to contribute to the whole.

Being a manager requires you to do a lot besides video. In today's marketplace, to be a successful video department manager, you must have financial skills, people skills, be able to hire and fire, be able to read a financial statement and build a five- or ten-year forecast for your department, be able to interact with vice presidents and corporate officers about things that have little relationship to video and deal with the people problems of the employees you manage.

Top management may decide to put you in charge of a department, either because you have reached the upper limits of the pay scale or because you have proven yourself so successful at managing. Department manager jobs may include print, graphics, photography, slides, audiovisual, copy center, mail room, data processing, advertising, public relations or anything else they may want you to take charge of. Again, this takes more time away from what may be your first love—video.

Corporate video managers with tenure continually find that they spend less and less time in the control room and more and more time performing management duties. Much of their time is often unrelated to putting a good video production together.

Don't get me wrong. It may be that management is the right step for you. But beware of aspiring to something you are not really interested in. You are not a failure because of it.

Not everyone who took a management class should manage. And, in fact, most people who are successful managers will tell you that very few who manage should dare to call themselves successful.

Most video managers and department heads would tell you to look at all the parts of their job—not just the good parts. Hiring, firing, training, putting out fires, working late or on weekends, working on financial projections, payroll, employee hours, internal frictions and politics are just the tip of the iceberg for a manager. Be certain you know what you are getting into.

GETTING AHEAD WITHOUT GOING INTO MANAGEMENT

Yes, it is possible. But much of the reasoning and logic is for you to realize and then internalize. Early in this chapter, I indicated that many of the positions listed were ends unto themselves. A person who enjoys the role of a, say videographer, need not go beyond the title to progress in his or her work.

What follows are some ideas, guidelines, and thoughts that may help you to get ahead without becoming "the boss."

Enjoy Your Work

At the risk of sounding like a pop culture throwback from the 1960s, I do feel that the people who are truly happy are the people who like their work. Your enjoyment of what you do causes you to be stimulated and to look for more and different ways to do things. The happiest people in most organizations are not necessarily those who are forging ahead through office politics in order to become the next vice president. They are the people who really enjoy what they do and get satisfaction from a job well done.

A good attitude makes the job much easier and allows you to concentrate on what you do and how to do it better. For a cameraperson, not every shot has been done and not every subject or location has been interpreted by you.

For the editor, every story is a unique opportunity for your specialized treatment. And there are always plenty of things to try to make you better at what you do.

Generally, I have found that people are very satisfied in nonbroadcast television. I think this is due to the creative demands put on every person in every position. Nonbroadcast video professionals are not stuck with only thinking logically. Their visionary abilities are called upon in their work and allow them the freedom "to go off and produce" by themselves and in their own way. I think that human nature requires that "independence of mind" and the break that comes with it.

SET YOUR SAILS TOWARD YOUR GOAL

Probably, the most stable and happy people are those who have their goals firmly in mind. Rather than take what life gives them, they seem to know what they want out of life and arrive at it in a logical fashion.

The great inventors of our time all had the ability to set a goal and stick to it. While recently at Kodak Business Television in Rochester, NY, I was fascinated by the story of George Eastman and his resolve to find a dry negative process for photography and a way to put the art of photography in everyone's hands.

Likewise, if you set goals for yourself and divide those goals into logical "bite-sized" steps, you will find renewed interest in what you do and an increase in your drive to get things done.

Do you want that IABC Golden Quill Award for superb writing skills? Keep a copy of the entry form nearby. Keep those articles about last year's winners in your notebook. Get a list of past receivers of the award and see what it takes to achieve the gold.

I hope this does not sound silly because goal setting within your career is the one area where you have total control. And, when you attain your goals, you will have progressed further in your life than many who fill the CEO suites in this country.

INDEPENDENCE DAY

Freelancing is almost an industry unto itself. Born of necessity, fueled by economics, the freelancer has found the market hard to get into, but, once he or she does, it is well worth the effort. That is because freelancing, or the use of independents by nonbroadcast (and broadcast) television entities, is expanding at a great rate.

No one really knows how quickly the independent market is growing because freelancing is a relatively new phenomenon. A survey by ITVA of 219 independents revealed that over 78% of respondents had been freelancing for less than seven years.

Layoffs by the television networks and the related belt-tightening by network affiliates in the early 1980s force-fed the freelance market on the East and West Coasts. The proliferation of independent stations and cable services competing for the same number of television viewers combined with the corporate climate of takeover and merger (NBC and RCA by GE, ABC by Capital Cities, CBS in a takeover by Lawrence Tisch of Loew's Corporation) resulted in a more bottom-line mentality. Thus, many experienced production people were thrust out of jobs and into the independent arena.

Freelancing has also grown across the United States in response to the enormous expansion of the nonbroadcast television marketplace. And as the freelance community grows, corporations and institutions are finding that hiring freelancers provides flexibility and cost efficiency. It is a simple fact that most nonbroadcast departments have high- and low-water marks in production schedules. Although an investment in sophisticated equipment may require a concomitant investment in permanent personnel, the swing in the amount of production (and kinds of production) dictates the sane and sensible use of freelancers.

In fact, many video departments have a list of freelancers that they use on a consistent basis. Freelancers, in turn, often have two or three major clients and a host of minor clients to parcel their services to. Nonbroadcast television departments enjoy the use of independents during their production high points and on specific productions; the freelancers enjoy their freedom and increased income. The rate paid to freelancers is usually higher than that paid to permanent employees. However, freelancers must do without some benefits—health insurance, paid vacation time, etc.—that staff employees take for granted. The freelancer must pay taxes and expenses. Also, he or she does *not* enjoy the stability of a regular paycheck.

The use of freelancers also benefits the clients. The higher rates charged by freelancers are more than offset by paying only for hours or days worked and the fact that no benefits are added to the base wage.

Compensation for freelancers varies greatly. Their fees are dependent on the services provided, experience-level of the freelancer and the geographical marketplace. The ITVA Salary Survey for 1988 indicated that slightly over 63% of the independents had gross billings between $15,000 and $100,000. Forty-seven percent indicated net profits of $15,000 to $50,000.

Types of freelancers vary greatly. In the ITVA survey, independents classified themselves as (listed in order of greatest number): producer, one-person operation, writer, videographer, director, manager, editor, audiovisual specialist, assistant producer, technician, engineer and production assistant.

Obviously, the profit-based side of nonbroadcast television provides many opportunities for freelancers. Institutions do not have the budget or flexibility to hire freelancers as frequently as corporations, for-profit hospitals and medical centers, utilities, cable companies, advertising companies, public relations firms and production houses do.

Freelancing takes many forms. There are videographers, editors, producers, lighting gaffers, writers and directors. Many types of jobs overlap. Freelancers can work one day for a nonbroadcast television corporation and spend the next day working with a broadcast crew.

Some freelancers enter the field from full-time positions; others are thrust into it because they cannot seem to find permanent employment. Some freelancers view their independent status as an interim step in their quest for permanent employment. Others feel that freelancing is a natural progression and the ultimate step in their careers.

In actuality, it is too early to determine whether freelancing is a permanent section of the television industry or, as has been suggested, only an aberration that is the result of too many bodies for too few positions. Some critics see corporate America's zest for the freelance industry as a way to add staff while minimizing costs. Freelancing exists, they say, because people are willing to be exploited, and business is more than willing to exploit them.

Prospects for Freelancers

Nonbroadcast areas that seem most open for freelancers include the corporate and production-house arenas. That is largely because these sectors are based on the profit motive. Hospital and medical areas that produce programming for resale are also hot areas for freelancers. As the videoconference area grows, the need for freelance production and engineering personnel is increasing. In terms of pure increase, this area may be the greatest growth area in the coming years.

Cable television has always used freelancers to augment its staffs. However, cable television is in a state of flux because of deregulation and the proliferation of MSOs. While the need for freelancers will grow, the extent of growth largely depends on the influences of deregulation and MSOs on the industry.

Some freelancers are concerned about their ability to move back into permanent jobs later in their careers. Finding a permanent position in nonbroadcast television depends on the freelancer's depth and quality of experience. On the positive side, freelancers usually know the market and may have made many professional contacts with the very people who might employ them. On the negative side, freelancers may have trouble adjusting to the confines of a structured organization. Because non-salary benefits (medical coverage, stock options, etc.) can add up to an estimated 40% of a permanent employee's compensation, full-time positions often offer less money than the freelancer can make in the open market.

Freelance Pros and Cons

A person contemplating freelancing has to be coldly realistic about marketplace opportunities and the realities of being self-employed.

Freelancers must be motivated. If you do not go and get the business, it is not going to come and get you. (Forget the stories that you have heard about everyone beating a path to your door because you are good. They are just not true!)

Permanent positions may seem to pay much less than your daily rate. Some freelancers turn down $30,000-a-year positions because if they work 40 hours per week, each and every week, they will make $50,000 a year. This can be the case. But what if you hit a lull and do not work for three weeks? What if you get two offers for the same time and must turn down one? The client you could not service may decide to live without you forever.

Medical coverage is an important aspect of permanent employment. Most businesses have at least adequate health coverage. Some businesses have fantastic health plans that include eyeglasses, prescriptions and dental care. What if you get sick for a month or more? And if you get sick, did you think to buy health insurance for yourself? (Self-employed individuals can only purchase health insurance at greatly increased rates. Insurance companies charge more for single policyholders than they do for group insurance.) If you get sick while on a remote in North Carolina, who's going to pay medical costs, who's going to get you to the hospital and take over the jobs you are going to miss while you are laid up?

As a freelancer, it is of the utmost importance that you find and retain qualified tax accounting and legal advice. Do not retain friends of friends or relatives, but professionals who understand what you are doing. Their advice will save you money in the long run. The Internal Revenue Service and other legal entities will have you for lunch if your books are not in order or if you have not filed Social Security and other taxes on time and in full. If you are audited by the IRS, hire a qualified tax attorney. The law has changed considerably and you will come out ahead with adequate representation. Your lawyer will also help you set up and do the legal things you must do as a sole proprietor/freelancer. He or she will also be around if you need to take clients to court or should someone sue you. Make no mistake—it can be a cold cruel world out there.

Be realistic about what you can earn as a freelancer and be overcautious about expenses. If you do not really need to buy a camera and VCR for remote recordings, then don't buy them. If you rent editing bays locally, then do not buy your own. Keep the money you would spend on equipment and supplies in your savings account and always explore renting or borrowing equipment rather than buying. The IRS has eliminated the investment credits that made such purchases advantageous in the past.

Freelancers must guard their time. You cannot do much charity work or donate your time because once it is known that you will do it, all philanthropic organizations will want your services. You are in a business that has a very small margin for error or waste. Spend your time productively by marketing yourself or developing other talents.

The Decision to Freelance

Before making the break and declaring yourself a freelancer or consultant:

- Be certain that there is a market for what you have to sell. If you are contemplating freelance writing services, be sure that there is enough of a need *before* you become independent.

- Read up on what it takes to operate an independent business. Talk to others who have done it before and get their advice.
- Be careful and remember that there are no sure things in life. Federal statistics show that two-thirds of all new businesses fail in their first year of operation, so be careful out there.

OTHER AVENUES TO PURSUE

We all get in ruts in our lives every now and then. The lack of progress you may feel in your job may be real or you may just be imagining it. That is, the way you look at things has a lot to with how you feel about them.

You can avoid such dead ends by taking the initiative and finding other avenues of expression for your work. Often, we like what we do, but we just get tired of the tedium, no matter how exciting our job is. We look at the grass and imagine it being greener on the other side of the job fence. Anyone who has left a job for another only to wish for their old one back will tell you that your career progress is a personal thing.

With that in mind, here are some ideas to try that will add to your work and pull you out of the rut.

Teach

Others can benefit from what you know. Maybe the local adult education center, college or university could benefit from your expertise. Perhaps teaching a workshop for interested people or a seminar at the local ITVA or IABC chapter would add meaning to your career. Imparting knowledge helps others, makes you feel good and keeps the information flowing.

Write

There are more industry magazines and newsletters now than ever before. And, as the field grows, there will be even more. When you start to write, read the magazine carefully and write about what you know. Down the road, you may also be tempted to impart knowledge by writing a book.

Consult Part-Time

Nothing helps you gain knowledge more quickly while helping others than consulting. You may be able to help a department get its feet off the ground or help institute a new service or program. Imparting your knowledge while consulting lets you know how others think and how organizations operate.

Network

It seems so easy, but it takes effort to attend professional meetings, seminars and conventions. Talking with other people gets the juices flowing and helps you see things through other eyes. Getting together with fellow editors or writers allows you to compare notes and think of new ways to approach problems. If someone else has tried a new technique and been successful with it, you may have an opportunity to try it later.

While networking, it does not hurt to visit other facilities and people. Often, it will give you greater insight into your job and organization. My wife, Joan, is a corporate television editor. Even though she has come a long way in her career, sometimes the "maybe I should change my job" blues hit. When they do, I've noticed that she brings up stories that she has heard while networking. "Well," she'll say about other organizations, "I could never put up with that . . . or with him as a boss." Again, her familiarity with other corporate television departments helps to dispel the grass-is-greener myth and makes her assessment of her career clearer.

CONCLUSION

What you are qualified for depends on what you have to offer a potential employer. You can control your own destiny and make timely moves through the nonbroadcast video career ladder. The next step is up to you, but it should be planned and made by gaining experience in the position you seek.

Not all people should aspire to be managers. In fact, this is one industry where staying in one job can provide a satisfying career. There are things, like teaching, freelancing, setting up your own business, writing and networking, that can help you grow without necessarily changing jobs. Decide upon your goals early. Then you can do the things necessary to move ahead.

10
Moving Out of Nonbroadcast Video

Professionals in nonbroadcast television—an information-processing field that is highly technological—sometimes "burn out" or simply want to change career paths and leave the field. And, in an industry that demands as much as ours does, career ladders in nonbroadcast video often lead away from the field as well as within it.

Nonbroadcast video experience qualifies you to make *many* diverse career moves. As with any job change, it requires you to assess your work history experience and determine what you have done that can benefit employers outside the industry.

You should take a hard, cold look at the areas you intend to move into. And you need to inventory your skills to successfully compete for the job you want.

If you feel that it is time to change career direction, but wonder whether your nonbroadcast background has prepared you for the step, chances are it has, you just have not thought of your background in such a context.

Many "nonbroadcasters" go on to jobs in other industries and do quite well. For some, the move is a welcome change of pace that helps renew their lives as well as careers. For others, it is just a brief respite that helps them redirect their energies and focus their career paths. Some return to the industry with renewed vigor. Others are just as glad to be gone.

WHAT CAN YOU DO?

People who are thinking of leaving an industry they have been in for a while fall into the trap of thinking they cannot do anything else and therefore are not valuable to anyone else. This is the kind of thinking that makes unhappy people stay in their jobs when they could be more content and productive doing something else.

Sit down and list your qualities. Then back them up with specific experiences you have had. Then, decide how those qualities can benefit you in other fields.

For example, if you enjoy writing and creating, but you are tired of writing scripts, your skills may adapt well to the print industry.

Are you good at starting different projects and meeting new people? Are you well organized, but want a little more freedom and money? Sales and marketing may be in your future.

Do you like knowing how things work, problem solving, troubleshooting, taking apart and fixing equipment? Engineering may be your direction.

Many nonbroadcast experiences can relate directly to other careers. The remainder of this chapter explores areas that non-broadcast personnel have moved to with a large degree of success.

ADVERTISING

Advertising agencies produce programs (although only 10-, 20- or 30-seconds long), deal with clients and exist in the business world to help others communicate. They often utilize some of the same production houses that nonbroadcast video organizations do. They often belong to the same professional groups and interact with nonbroadcast people. Because much of the work is similar, advertising is an area that nonbroadcast video people can enter with a good degree of success.

Advertising thrives on creativity and drive. If you have both, making the jump should be no problem. If, in your background, you have the ability to interact with a variety of people, to work on several different projects at the same time, to meet deadlines and always feel that you must take on more than you can ever do, then advertising can be a successful change for you.

You don't have to live in New York to be in advertising, although it is the largest advertising center. It is estimated that there are over 8000 advertising agencies throughout the United States.[1]

Advertising utilizes the various media—print, photography, graphics, audiovisual, radio and television—to persuade people to do something. The company or organization that wants a certain message out is the one that pays for the advertising. Advertising agencies, either independent or in-house departments, are responsible for doing the research, test marketing, idea development, concept implementation and follow-up research to prove that what was advertised reached its target audience.

Where to Look

There are advertising agencies and corporate advertising departments in virtually every market in the nation. Agencies usually service several clients while corporate departments function as either an in-house agency that services one account, or as the liaison between the outside agency and corporate management.

The Standard Directory of Advertising Agencies, known as the Red Book,[2] lists thousands of agencies and their regional offices. Larger agencies often have several offices to service regional or local accounts in many different cities.

---

[1] Shonan F. R. Noronha, *Careers in Communications* (Lincolnwood, IL: National Textbook Co., 1987), p. 102.
[2] Published every February, June and October by National Register Publishing Co. (Wilmette, IL).

The local Ad Club should also be able to help you find out who and where the agencies and in-house departments are.

Who Do They Hire?

Advertising agencies employ research assistants, account representatives, media buyers, copywriters, media coordinators, media supervisors, traffic managers, graphic artists, advertising assistants, art directors, television directors and ad managers.

Prerequisites

Good writing skills coupled with the ability to work with others while expressing your ideas are basic requirements. Most advertising people have degrees in advertising, marketing, business, management or communications. Should you have a degree in one area, practical experience is necessary in the others.

Freelancers are used by advertising agencies; this may be one way to get your foot in the door to a new career. People with production skills, such as producers, directors, writers and others, are used by advertising agencies to augment their in-house staffs.

PUBLIC RELATIONS

Rather than the creation and placement of advertisements about a specific product or service, public relations is generally more concerned with the type and amount of information released to the public about companies, organizations and industries.

For example, a hospital may stage an ad campaign aimed at increasing the number of people who use the hospital. It may feature paid advertisements describing new equipment, practices and doctors. But a more subtle and effective way to get the word out would be through public relations. PR might persuade the local news media to cover the opening of a new wing of the hospital or arrange for the local press to interview the new hospital administrator or head of surgery. Providing source material to the press on health and medical stories would be another PR strategy.

The U.S. Bureau of Labor statistics revealed that over 140,000 people are now in the field of public relations.

Being in PR requires you to be organized and able to get along with a number of people inside both organizations and the media. Communicating an organization's message through news placement may seem easy, but it takes a certain skill to know what news organizations deem worthy as news and what they think is simply a search for free publicity.

Where the true PR person shows his or her mettle is when the chips are down. For example, if you are working for an industry that has a negative image with the public, you have your hands full.

PR people should like to work with statistics because news organizations cannot seem to get enough of them. Therefore, the ability to develop and administer surveys is frequently necessary.

Where to Look

Advertising agencies usually have a related organization that serves as a PR firm. In addition, there are many separate PR firms that have no affiliation with an ad agency. The local chapter of the Public Relations Society of America (PRSA, 845 Third Ave., New York, NY 10022) should be able to help you find and meet PR firms and representatives.

The United States government is one of the largest employers of information officers, press secretaries, PR specialists and communications experts. Corporations have public relations staff to help both internal employee PR and external press PR.

Numerous nonprofit organizations, educational institutions, and hospitals have PR staffs to coordinate the dissemination of information.

Who Do They Hire?

Some of the jobs found in public relations include writers, assistants, researchers, account executives, supervisors and directors. Naturally, the higher you go up the ladder, the more management skills are required. Speech writers and event organizers will also find their niches in PR.

Prerequisites

A college degree in communications, management, journalism or speech is a good foundation. You should have experience in both oral and written communications. Ascending the PR career ladder will take experience in management, planning and marketing. A PR person must relate to many different people while keeping the main mission firmly in mind.

BROADCAST TELEVISION

When nonbroadcast television started, many of its pioneers were broadcast production and supervisory personnel. Broadcast producers, directors, writers and production personnel moved to nonbroadcast television to staff the then-new field. Because of this initial infusion of talent, the two fields have always enjoyed a communal talent pool. This crossover is most evident among acting talent and freelancers; people may work on a nonbroadcast video project one day and then participate in a shoot for a broadcast station the next day.

As cable television, independent stations (those without network affiliation) and even new networks (like the Fox network) grow, demand for programming to fill hours of operation has expanded. And as the demand for programming grows, so does the need for production personnel to produce the additional programs. As "station" personnel are often committed, these needs have opened the broadcast market to experienced professionals as never before.

Over 1600 television stations (including the newer low-power stations) exist throughout the country. Of them, one-third are educational stations (PBS), while the balance are commercial stations. Most commercial stations are affiliated with a network (ABC, NBC and CBS) and provide news, sports and local programs.

Independent stations with no network affiliation initially relied on reruns of old shows and movies for their programming. A buying and selling splurge of these independent stations occurred in the late 1970s and early 1980s. As a result, the quality of independent programming has approached that of the network affiliates. Many now produce original programming; some started their own news programs and covered local sports, and others started producing their own informational and entertainment programs.

Who Do They Hire?

Stations need professionals at every level. They rely on news directors, program producers, videographers, production assistants, graphic artists, engineers, writers, editors, audio engineers, master control operators, technical directors, videotape technicians, gaffers, lighting directors, set designers, makeup artists, talent coordinators, assistant producers, floor managers and assistant directors.

Broadcast stations often have the benefit of owning the latest equipment, but they also are more rigid in their structure. This creates an opposite situation from nonbroadcast television and results in camerapersons working *only* with the camera, audio engineers working *only* with audio equipment, and news directors *only* directing the news.

Prerequisites

Broadcast video positions usually require people to operate efficiently under deadlines. If the piece you are working on is needed for the 6:00 news, then it has to be done and in master control to run at that time.

Your work experience must be high quality. There is no time for training, and your allowable margin of error is slight. The videographer who misses the shot of the burning building may find himself unemployed.

Positions are clearly defined in broadcast television, much as they are in advertising and public relations. Production personnel do just that—produce programs. Directors and producers often have some management responsibility, but the lines between management, production, engineering and sales are tightly drawn. You are not encouraged to cross them.

Experience in television production coupled with a four-year degree in communications or a related field is necessary for most production positions. Management and sales positions can be filled by people with prior successful experience in related fields.

Where to Look

A complete annual listing of all television stations may be found in *Broadcasting-Cablecasting Yearbook*. *Broadcasting* magazine, published weekly, has an employment marketplace in the back of each issue listing hundreds of job openings.[3] It's also the bible of the industry and is a good way for you to learn about the field. Information may also be obtained from the National Association of Broadcasters (1771 North Street NW, Washington, DC 20036).

---

[3] *Broadcasting-Cablecasting Yearbook* and *Broadcasting* are published by Broadcasting Publications, Inc. (Washington, DC).

RADIO AND AUDIO STUDIOS

There are over 10,000 radio stations throughout the United States. I guess I'm partial to radio, because it was the place I started my career. Later, after I worked at two different stations, I began my career in nonbroadcast television.

Radio is often overlooked as an area in which to either get started or move into from nonbroadcast. One of the reasons may be that radio is often looked at as television's older and lesser brother. It is a misconception because radio and audio production are an industry and an art unto themselves.

Radio incorporates many of the same qualities as video. Like television, program ideas are proposed, assessed and acted on. Segments are written, produced and edited. Programs are distributed and heard by both mass and select audiences. And, like video, evaluations are used to determine a program's effectiveness.

Radio is, after all, video without pictures. Because it is, many of the positions available in radio parallel those in video.

Radio is often an easier job market to enter than video for two reasons. First, most colleges de-emphasize its importance. (It's not really their fault. Students are naturally more interested in video production than audio, and schools tend to cater to students' demands.) Second, because radio is with us everywhere— in the home, car, at work—we tend to take it for granted and overlook it as a career move.

Where to Look

Broadcasting magazine lists several radio and audio production openings weekly. You can get a complete list of all the radio stations in your area by looking in the *Broadcasting-Cablecasting*

Yearbook. The National Association of Broadcasters can also supply you with career information on the radio industry. Another possible source of information is National Public Radio. They are poor, but do hire a lot of temporary workers (2025 M Street NW, Washington, DC 20036).

Who Do They Hire?

Audio technicians, sales personnel, management, announcers, news directors, news reporters, engineers, scriptwriters, traffic personnel, program managers and program producers are needed in radio. Recording studios often have positions for audio editors, engineers, music directors and related personnel.

Prerequisites

A four-year degree in communications with an emphasis in radio is the minimum requirement. Good interpersonal communications skills are necessary for audio production combined with an understanding of the equipment and medium. Announcers need professional vocal skills; experience in theater, debate and speech can help greatly.

Many smaller stations require their personnel to perform many functions. For example, in smaller markets it is not unusual for on-air talent to help sell advertising time for their shows. It is also not unusual for them to engineer and produce their own programs. Therefore, the abilities to adapt to changing situations, to work under deadlines and to do many different things will enhance your chances in radio and audio studios.

OTHER ENDEAVORS

There is no limit to what you can do with your successful background and experiences in nonbroadcast television. You may want to strike out on your own and set up your own business. That business may or may not be related to video. But the skills and techniques acquired in nonbroadcast television should have groomed you to be successful at a number of different things.

Creativity allows you to see things from many different angles. You may go into other areas of art, or you may use your creative talents for problem solving or building a new career.

The ability to work with others will allow you to work with people in a number of ways—perhaps operating your own business, managing a company or division unrelated to video, or counseling others.

Nonbroadcast television's close ties to business allow you to learn about profit and nonprofit organizations. You will not rise through the ranks of nonbroadcast television without learning about accounting, balancing a budget, liabilities, assets, depreciation and other business concepts.

Data processing experience—in word processing, spreadsheet analysis, graphics, local area networks, editors, digital effects and character generators—gives the nonbroadcast person an additional edge in today's economy. Computers are the lifeblood of industry. People who can use computers have a decided advantage.

What I have tried to point out is that, in the nonbroadcast industry, you have opportunities to gain experience (i.e., leadership, accounting, data processing) that can help you to move into other fields. And much like your initial steps to find a new job, moving out requires you to take an inventory of your background, assess your assets and deficiencies, work to gain experience in areas that you are lacking in and then plan your move.

THE STATURE OF NONBROADCAST TELEVISION

In the early years of the industry, nonbroadcast video employees were considered technical people, or "techies." A "techie" was someone who had specific technical skills that were not considered to be transferable to other fields. In the last 10 years, nonbroadcast professionals have improved their career visibility by broadening their experiences and showing that they are capable of much more than the technical operation of equipment.

As the importance of communications within business, government and institutions has increased, so has the stature of the people who administer them.

Nonbroadcast professionals have found that, with the proper mix of experience, self-promotion, politics and hard work, they are capable of moving to the top of their field— or out and into other career areas.

APPENDIX A: ORGANIZATIONS THAT ACTIVELY USE VIDEO

ALABAMA

Alabama Power Co.
600 N. 18th St.
Birmingham, AL 35291

Teledyna Brown Engineering
M.S. 172 Cummings Research
Huntsville, AL 35807

Vanity Fair Mills, Inc.
Management Devel.
624 S. Alabama Ave.
Monroeville, AL 36462

ALASKA

Sealaska Corp.
Corp. Comm.
One Sealaska Plaza, #400
Juneau, AK 99801

Standard Alaska Production Co.
Standard Oil
Graphic Arts
PO Box 196612
Anchorage, AK 99519

ARIZONA

Arizona Game & Fish Dept.
2222 W. Greenway Rd.
Phoenix, AZ 85023

Greyhound Corp.
111 W. Clarendon Sta. 2201
Phoenix, AZ 85077

Valley National Bank
A/V Svces.
PO Box 71, 241 N. Central Ave.
Phoenix, AZ 85001

ARKANSAS

Arkansas Power and Light Co.
PO Box 551
Little Rock, AR 72203

Tyson Foods, Inc.
PO Drawer E
Springdale, AR 72764

Wal-Mart Stores, Inc.
Dept. of Trng. & Devel.
PO Box 116
Bentonville, AR 72716

CALIFORNIA

Amdahl Corp.
1250 E. Arques, M/S 301
Sunnyvale, CA 94088

Apple Computer
10455 Bandley Dr.
Cupertino, CA 95014

Avery Label Co.
777 E. Foothill Blvd.
Azusa, CA 91702

Beatrice/Hunt-Wesson, Inc.
1645 W. Valencia Dr.
Fullerton, CA 92634

Note: The organizations listed in Appendix A were selected from *The Video Register and Teleconferencing Resources Directory, 1988*, published by Knowledge Industry Publications, Inc.

Del Monte Corp.
PO Box 3575
One Market Plaza
San Francisco, CA 94119

General Dynamics/Convair
PO Box 161018
San Diego, CA 92116

Glendale Federal Savings
201 W. Lexington Ave.
Glendale, CA 91209

GTE Sprint
Marketing Services
500 Airport Blvd., #422
Burlingame, CA 94010

Hughes Aircraft Co.
A/V Center
1901 W. Malvern St.
Fullerton, CA 92634

Kaiser Permanente Medical Care
3900 Broadway–Bldg. 2
Oakland, CA 94611

Lawrence Livermore National Lab.
PO Box 808 L-699; Bldg. 003
Livermore, CA 94550

Levi Strauss & Co.
Levi's Plaza, PO Box 7215
San Francisco, CA 94120

Longs Drug Stores
Training Dept.
141 N. Civic Dr.
Walnut Creek, CA 94596

Mattel Toy Co., Inc.
Visual Services
5150 W. Rosecrans Ave.
Hawthorne, CA 90250

May Co.
May Co. Department Stores
6160 Laurel Canyon Blvd.
North Hollywood, CA 91606

Mervyn's
Dayton-Hudson Corp.
25001 Industrial Blvd.
Hayward, CA 94545

Nissan Motor Corp. U.S.A.
Natl. Sales Training Comm.
PO Box 191
Gardena, CA 90247

Northrop Corp.
Electro-Mechanical Div.
500 E. Orangethorpe
Anaheim, CA 92801

Ralphs Grocery Co.
Federated Dept. Stores
TV Dept.
1100 W. Artesia Blvd.
Compton, CA 90220

Redken Laboratories Inc.
A/V Dept.
6625 Variel Ave.
Canoga Park, CA 91303

Rolm MIL-SPEC Computers
1 River Oaks Pl., 166
San Jose, CA 95134

Security Pacific Bank
Communicating Arts
333 S. Beaudry, W16-75
Los Angeles, CA 90017

Shaklee Corp.
Shaklee Vision, T-291
444 Market St.
San Francisco, CA 94111

Unisys Corp.
Organizational Development
25725 Jeronimo Rd., MS 125
Mission Viejo, CA 92630

Wells Fargo Bank
Comm. Arts
111 Sutter St., 4th Floor
San Francisco, CA 94104

COLORADO

Adolph Coors. Co.
Corporate Television
Mail #NH 140
Golden, CO 80401

Digital Equipment Corp.
Educational Services
301 Rockrimmon Blvd., S.
Colorado Springs, CO 80919

IBM Corp.
Information Products Div.
PO Box 1900
Boulder, CO 80302

Mountain Bell
U.S. West
Training and Educ.
3898 S. Teller, Rm. 156
Lakewood, CO 80235

Rockwell International
Rocky Flats Plant, PO Box 464
Golden, CO 80401

United Airlines Flight Center
Stapleton International Airport
Denver, CO 80207

United Bank of Denver
United Banks of Colorado
Visual Comm.
1700 Broadway
Denver, CO 80274

CONNECTICUT

Cuisinart
15 Valley Dr.
Greenwich, CT 06836

Ethan Allen Inc.
Educ. and Training Dept.
Ethan Allen Dr.
Danbury, CT 06810

GTE
1 Stamford Forum
Stamford, CT 06904

Hartford Insurance Group
A/V Svces.
Hartford Plaza
Hartford, CT 06115

Heublein, Inc.
Grand Metropolitan PLC
A/V Dept.
330 New Park Ave.
Hartford, CT 06142

Otis Elevator North American
Communications Dept.
1 Farm Springs
Farmington, CT 06032

Pratt & Whitney Aircraft
United Technologies Corp.
400 Main St.
East Hartford, CT 06108

Travellers Insurance Co.
1 Tower Square
Hartford, CT 06183

Union Carbide Corp.
Media Prod. Services
39 Old Ridgebury Rd.
Danbury, CT 06817

DELAWARE

Amtrak Passenger Corp.
Foot of Vandever Ave.
Wilmington, DE 19801

E.I. Dupont De Numours Co.
External Affairs Dept.
1111 Tatnall St., TG-1
Wilmington, DE 19898

DISTRICT OF COLUMBIA

American Red Cross
National Hdqtrs.
Washington, DC 20006

GEICO
Communications
5260 Western Ave. N.W.
Washington, DC 20076

Smithsonian Institution
Office of Telecommunications
MHA, Rm. BB-40
14th St. & Constitution Ave.
Washington, DC 20560

U.S. Government Printing Office
Visual Comm. Section
N. Capital & H. Sts. N.W.
Washington, DC 20401

Woodward & Lothrop
Video Center
11 and F Sts. N.W.
Washington, DC 20013

FLORIDA

Burdine's
Federated Dept. Stores
22 E. Flagler St., 4th Fl.
Miami, FL 33131

Eastern Airlines, Inc.
Video Support Svces.
Bldg. 30, Rm. 105, MIAFX
Miami, FL 33148

Maas Brothers
Allied Stores Corp.
Trng. and Devel. Dept.
PO Box 311
Tampa, FL 33601

Pan American World Airways
PO Box 592096 PAF65
Miami, FL 33159

Publix Super Markets, Inc.
PO Box 407
Lakeland, FL 33802

Ryder Truck Rental, Inc.
Ryder System, Inc.
Learning Center
3600 N.W. 82nd Ave.
Miami, FL 33166

GEORGIA

Coca-Cola U.S.A.
Media Services
PO Drawer 1734
Atlanta, GA 30301

Geogia-Pacific Corp.
Georgia-Pacific TV
133 Peachtree St., N.E.
Atlanta, GA 30303

Rich's
Federated Dept. Stores
Video Communications Dept. 909
PO Box 4539
Atlanta, GA 30302

West Point—Pepperell, Inc.
Employee Communications Dept.
PO Box 71
West Point, GA 31833

HAWAII

First Interstate Bank of Hawaii
1314 S. King St.
Honolulu, HI 96814

Hawaiian Electric Co.
Corp. Communications
PO Box 2750
Honolulu, HI 96840

IDAHO

Bureau of Land Management
12019 La Pan Dr.
Boise, ID 83709

Idaho First National Bank
Moore Financial
PO Box 8247
Boise, ID 83733

ILLINOIS

Abbott Laboratories
Hospital Div.
Abbott Park
North Chicago, IL 60064

American Hospital Co.
1450 Waukegan Rd.
McGaw Park, IL 60085

AMOCO Corp.
Audiovisual Services
200 E. Randolph Dr., MC 2504
Chicago, IL 60601

Baxter-Travenol Laboratories
1 Baxter Pkwy.
Deerfield, IL 60015

Deltak Training Corp.
E.-W. Technological Center
Naperville, IL 60540

Fiatallis
Video Productions
245 E. North Ave.
Carol Stream, IL 60188

Hickory Ridge Conference Center
AT&T Resource Mgmt.
Business Services
1195 Summerhill Dr.
Lisle, IL 60532

Jewel Food Stores, Inc.
A/V Training Svces.
1955 W. North Ave.
Melrose Park, IL 60160

Maremont Corp.
Arvin Ind.
Training/Dev.
250 E. Kehoe Blvd.
Carol Stream, IL 60188

Marshall Field's
BATUS, Inc.
Visual Communications Dept.
111 N. State St.
Chicago, IL 60690

Military Airlift Command
USAF
MAC/PAL
Hdqtrs. MAC/PAMA
Scott Air Force Base, IL 62225

Montgomery Ward & Co., Inc.
Montgomery Ward Pl., 8-A
Chicago, IL 60671

Quaker Oats Co.
345 Merchandise Mart
Chicago, IL 60654

Sargent & Lundy Engineers
Employee Services– Training
55 E. Monroe St.
Chicago, IL 60603

Sherwin-Williams Co.
Mktg. Comm.
11541 S. Champlain Ave.
Chicago, IL 60628

Stauffer Chemical Co.
Eleventh & Arnold Sts.
Chicago Heights, IL 60411

Sundstrand Aviation Operations
Sundstrand Corp.
Graphic Communications
4747 Harrison Ave., PO Box 700
Rockford, IL 61125

Wickes Furniture
Wickes Cos., Inc.
Communication Svces.
351 W. Dundee Rd.
Wheeling, IL 60090

World Book Inc.
Scott-Fetzer
Trng. & Recruiting
Merchandise Mart Plaza
Chicago, IL 60654

INDIANA

Cummins Engine Co.
PO Box 3005; MC11B13
Columbus, IN 47202

Eli Lilly & Co.
Marketing Comm.
307 E. McCarty St.
Indianapolis, IN 46285

GTE Midwestern Telephone
PO Box 407; HQ 19845 North US
Westfield, IN 46074

Hurco Manufacturing Co., Inc.
A/V Advertising
PO Box 68/180; 6460 Faguaro Ct.
Indianapolis, IN 46268

Miles Laboratories, Inc.
Bayer, AG
1127 Myrtle St.
Elkhart, IN 46514

IOWA

Farm Bureau Insurance
Agency Devel. Dept.
5400 University Ave.
West Des Moines, IA 50265

Fisher Controls International
Monsanto
Media Center
205 S. Center St.
Marshalltown, IA 50158

The Maytag Co.
Field Educ. Dept.
One Dependability Sq.
Newton, IA 50208

KANSAS

Boeing Military Airplane Co.
Employee Devel.
PO Box 7730
Wichita, KS 67277

Pizza Hut, Inc.
9111 E. Douglas
Wichita, KS 67207

Sterling Drugs
1776 N. Centennial Dr.
McPherson, KS 67460

KENTUCKY

Ashland Oil, Inc.
PO Box 391
Ashland, KY 41114

Kentucky Fried Chicken
PO Box 32070
Louisville, KY 40232

LOUISIANA

Louisiana Office of Tourism
Louisiana State Gov't.
Culture, Recreation & Tourism
94291
Baton Rouge, LA 70804

McDermott International, Inc.
1010 Common St.
New Orleans, LA 70160

MAINE

Eastern Maine Medical Center
Education Svces. Div.
489 State St.
Bangor, ME 04401

Union Mutual
A/V Resources
2211 Congress St.
Portland, ME 04122

MARYLAND

CSX Corp.
CSX Creative Services
100 N. Charles St. 805
Baltimore, MD 21201

Kelly-Springfield Tire Co.
Goodyear Tire & Rubber Co.
PO Box 300
Cumberland, MD 21502

Marriott Corp.
Employee Comm./Creative Svces.
10400 Fernwood Rd.
Bethesda, MD 20817

Tracor Applied Sciences, Inc.
Tracor, Inc.
Dev. Systems Dept.
2 Pine Hill Center, Box 600
Lexington Park, MD 20653

MASSACHUSETTS

Millipore Corp.
80 Ashby Rd.
Bedford, MA 01730

Monsanto
Saflex Dept.
730 Worcester St.
Indian Orchard, MA 01108

New England Telephone
NYNEX
TV Center
185 Franklin St., Rm. 310
Boston, MA 02107

Raytheon Co.
Hartwell Rd.
Bedford, MA 01730

Zayre Corp.
A/V Production Svces.
Framingham, MA 01701

MICHIGAN

AC Spark Plug
General Motors Corp.
1300 Dort Hwy.
Flint, MI 48556

Amway Corp.
7575 E. Fulton Rd.
Ada, MI 49355

Applicon
Education Dept.
4251 Plymouth Rd.
Ann Arbor, MI 48106

Buick Motor Division
General Motors Corp.
902 E. Hamilton Ave.
Flint, MI 48550

Chrysler Corp.
Chrysler Motors
Chrysler Video Ctr.
3675 E. Outer Dr.
Detroit, MI 48234

C.P.C. Group
General Motors Corp.
Video Center
32327 Crestwood La.
Fraser, MI 48026

Dow Corning Corp.
A/V Comm.
PO Box 0994
Midland, MI 48686

Ford Motor Co.
Broadcast News Dept.
The American Rd., Rm. 906 PO B
Dearborn, MI 48121

Kellogg Co.
One Kellogg Square
Battle Creek, MI 49016

Meijer Inc.
Personnel Dept.
4411 Plainfield N.E.
Grand Rapids, MI 49505

Pontiac Motor Div.
1 Pontiac Plaza
Pontiac, MI 48058

Unisys Corp.
Corporate Communications
One Unisys Place
Detroit, MI 48232

MINNESOTA

Dayton Hudson Dept. Store
Dayton Hudson Corp.
Studio Eleven
701 Industrial Blvd.
Minneapolis, MN 55413

Deluxe Check Printers, Inc.
A/V Services
1080 W. County Rd. F
St. Paul, MN 55126

General Mills, Inc.
PO Box 1113, 9200 Wayzata Blvd.
Minneapolis, MN 55440

Honeywell, Inc.
Corporate Film Svces.
Honeywell Plaza, 2701 4th Ave. S.
Minneapolis, MN 55408

Mayo Clinic
A/V Center
Plummer Bldg.
Rochester, MN 55905

MISSISSIPPI

Deposit Guaranty National Bank
PO Box 1200
Jackson, MS 39215

Mississippi Bureau of Marine
    Resources
PO Drawer 959
Long Beach, MS 39560

MISSOURI

Anheuser-Busch Cos., Inc.
Busch Creative Services Corp.
5240 Oakland Ave.
St. Louis, MO 63110

Monsanto Co.
800 N. Linbergh Blvd.
St. Louis, MO 63167

Payless Cashways Inc.
Media Services Dept.
300 W. 19th Terrace
Kansas City, MO 64108

Ralston-Purina Co.
900 Checkerboard Sq.
St. Louis, MO 63164

Venture Stores Inc.
May Co.
Organizational Development
2001 E. Terra Lane, PO Box 110
O'Fallon, MO 63366

MONTANA

Kampgrounds of America (KOA)
Video Production
550 N. 31st St.
Billings, MT 59101

Missoula County
Personnel & Labor Relations
200 W. Broadway
Missoula, MT 59801

NEBRASKA

Father Flanagan's Boys' Home
Public Relations
14100 Crawford St.
Boys Town, NE 68010

Mutual & United of Omaha
Mutual of Omaha Plaza
Omaha, NE 68175

Northwestern Bell
Public Relations Dept.
1314 Douglas on the Mall
Omaha, NE 68102

Union Pacific Railroad
A/V Services
1416 Dodge St.
Omaha, NE 68179

NEVADA

Aerospace Audiovisual Service
Detachment 3
1365 Audiovisual Squadron Nellis
Air Force Base
Las Vegas, NV 89191

University Medical Center
HRD A/V Services
1800 W. Charleston Blvd.
Las Vegas, NV 89101

NEW HAMPSHIRE

Markem Corp.
150 Congress St.
Keene, NH 03431

Sanders Associates
Education & Training Dept.
MER 24-1569 C.S. 2034
Nashua, NH 03061

NEW JERSEY

A-P-A Transport Corp.
2100 88th St.
North Bergen, NJ 07047

AT&T Bell Laboratories
Corporate Television
101 John F. Kennedy Pkwy.
Short Hills, NJ 07078

Chubb Corp.
Training and Education
15 Mountain View Rd.
Warren, NJ 07061

Ciba-Geigy Pharmaceutical Div.
Audio-Visual Center
584 Valley Rd.
Gillette, NJ 07933

Grand Union Co.
A/V Dept.
100 Broadway
Elmwood Park, NJ 07407

Hoechst-Roussel Pharmaceutical
American Hoechst Corp.
Trng. Dept.
Rte., 202/206 N
Somerville, NJ 08876

Hoffman La Roche Inc.
340 Kingsland Rd.
Nutley, NJ 07110

Macy's N.J.
Employee Communications
131 Market St.
Newark, NJ 07101

Merck Sharp & Dohme Int'l.
Merck & Co.
Advertising Dept.
126 E. Lincoln Ave.
Rahway, NJ 07065

Minolta Corp.
101 Williams Dr.
Ramsey, NJ 07446

Nabisco Brands, Inc.
AV/TV Center
7 Sylvan Way
Parsippany, NJ 07054

Ortho Pharmaceutical Corp.
Johnson and Johnson
Visual Communications
Rte. 202, PO Box 300
Raritan, NJ 08869

Squibb Corp.
Video AV Services
PO Box 4000
Princeton, NJ 08540

Warner-Lambert Co.
A/V Dept.
201 Tabor Rd.
Morris Plains, NJ 07950

NEW MEXICO

Sandia National Labs.
Education & Training Div. 3522
Box 5800
Albuquerque, NM 87185

U.S. Dept. of Energy
Electronic Systems Br.
PO Box 5400; Kirtland AFB
Albuquerque, NM 87115

NEW YORK

Agway Training Center
9 Adler Dr.
East Syracuse, NY 13057

American Express
Bank Div.
200 Vesey St.
World Financial Center
New York, NY 10285

Avon Products, Inc.
Avon Audio-Video Facility
Avon Video Network
9 W. 57th St.
New York, NY 10019

Big V Supermarkets, Inc.
ShopRite Supermarkets
Video Communications
176 N. Main St.
Florida, NY 10921

Chase Manhattan Bank
80 Pine St., Floor 21
New York, NY 10081

Dean Witter Reynolds, Inc.
Sears, Roebuck and Co.
Video Communications Center
5 World Trade Center
New York, NY 10048

Deloitte, Haskins & Sells
Video/A/V Svces.
1114 Ave. of the Americas
New York, NY 10036

Empire of America
Corp. Relations
1 Main Place
Buffalo, NY 14202

First Boston Corp.
509 Madison Ave., 10th Floor
New York, NY 10055

General Electric Co.
Turbine Mktg. and
    Projects Operations
1 River Rd., Bldg. 500-238
Schenectady, NY 12345

Lord & Taylor
May Co.
TV Studio
424 Fifth Ave.
New York, NY 10018

Macy's New York
151 W. 34th St.
New York, NY 10001

Manufacturers Hanover
Mgmt. Communications
270 Park Ave., Floor 11
New York, NY 10017

Memorial Sloan-Kettering
Biomedical Communications
1275 York Ave.
New York, NY 10021

Morgan Guaranty Trust Co.
Video/Teleconferencing Dept.
20 Pine St., 29th Floor
New York, NY 10015

OTB Communications Network
Capital District Regional OTB
510 Smith St.
Schenectady, NY 12305

Paine Webber
1285 Ave. of the Americas
New York, NY 10019

Price Waterhouse
1251 Ave. of the Americas
New York, NY 10020

Saks Fifth Avenue
BATUS, Inc.
Corp. Communications
611 Fifth Ave., Floor 9
New York, NY 10022

Sotheby's
1334 York Ave.
New York, NY 10021

Triborough Bridge & Tunnel
    Authority
Engineering Dept.
Randalls Island
New York, NY 10035

NORTH CAROLINA

Belk Dept. Stores
Belk Hensdale
4525 Camp Ground Rd.
Fayetteville, NC 28304

Hardee's Food Systems, Inc.
Imasco USA
Communication Svces.
1233 N. Church St.
Rocky Mount, NC 27801

R.J. Reynolds Tobacco USA
1100 Reynolds Blvd., CHQ, 1C
Winston-Salem, NC 27102

NORTH DAKOTA

Basin Electric Power Coop
Communication Services Division
1717 E. Interstate Ave.
Bismarck, ND 58501

North Dakota State Hospital
Staff Development Dept.
PO Box 476
Jamestown, ND 58401

OHIO

American Greetings Corp.
10500 American Rd.
Cleveland, OH 44144

Doehler-Jarvis/Farley Ind. Inc.
PO Box 902; 1945 Smead Ave.
Toledo, OH 43691

General Electric Co.
Specialty Materials Dept.
6325 Huntley Rd.
Worthington, OH 43085

Kitchenaid, Inc.
3800 Space Dr.
Dayton, OH 45414

Lazarus
Federated Department Stores
Video Comm.
Seventh & Race Sts.
Cincinnati, OH 45202

Liqui-Box Corp.
6950 Worthington-Galena Rd.
Worthington, OH 43085

Lubrizol Corp.
Product Promotion Dept.
29400 Lakeland Blvd.
Wickliffe, OH 44092

NCR
A/V Dept.
101 W. Schantz Ave.
Dayton, OH 45479

Roadway Express, Inc.
Roadway Services
Video Productions
1077 Gorge Blvd.
Akron, OH 44309

OKLAHOMA

Conoco Research
DuPont
Research Services Div.
7420 RDW
Ponca City, OK 74603

Liberty National Bank
Banks of Mid-America, Inc.
100 N. Broadway, PO Box 25848
Oklahoma City, OK 73125

Occidental Oil & Gas Corp.
Occidental Petroleum Corp.
AV-Video Dept.
Box 300, LL-10
Tulsa, OK 74102

OREGON

Freightliner Corp.
Daimler-Benz AG
4747 N. Channel Ave.
Portland, OR 97217

Meier & Frank Co.
May Department Stores Co.
Training Dept.
621 S.W. Fifth
Portland, OR 97204

Portland General Electric Co.
A/V Svces.
121 S.W. Salmon St.
Portland, OR 97204

U.S. Bancorp
Corporate Comm.
555 S.W. Oak St.
Portland, OR 97204

PENNSYLVANIA

Aluminum Co. of America
Communications Services
770 Alcoa Bldg.
Pittsburgh, PA 15219

ARA Services, Inc.
1101 Market St.
Philadelphia, PA 19107

Bethlehem Steel Corp.
Human Resources
Martin Tower, Rm. 8-201
Bethlehem, PA 18016

Cigna Corp.
Corporate Video Services
1600 Arch St.
Philadelphia, PA 19106

Hershey Foods Corp.
1025 Reese Ave.
Hershey, PA 17033

Kulicke & Soffa Industries, Inc.
Media Services Dept.
2101 Blair Mill Rd.
Willow Grove, PA 19090

PPG Industries, Inc.
One PPG Place
Pittsburgh, PA 15272

Smithkline Beckman Corp.
PO Box 7929
Philadelphia, PA 19101

Strawbridge & Clothier
Communications Dept.
801 Market St.
Philadelphia, PA 19105

RHODE ISLAND

CVS
1 CVS Dr.
Woonsocket, RI 02895

Fram Corp.
Allied Corp.
Audio Visual
55 Pawtucket Ave.
East Providence, RI 02916

SOUTH CAROLINA

L'eggs Products
1810 W. Irby St.
Florence, SC 29501

Sonoco Products Co.
Vid. Svces.
N. Second St.
Hartsville, SC 29550

SOUTH DAKOTA

Eros Data Center
Mundt Federal Bldg.
Sioux Falls, SD 57198

Rapid City Police Dept.
Audio/Visual Unit
300 Kansas City St.
Rapid City, SD 57701

TENNESSEE

International Paper Co.
Corporate Communication
6400 Poplar Ave.
Memphis, TN 38119

Magic Chef
740 King Edward Ave.
Cleveland, TN 37311

TEXAS

American Airlines Flight Academy
Audio Visual Center
PO Box 619617 MD 869
DFW Airport, TX 75261

Casa Bonita Inc.
Unigate Restaurants Inc.
Personnel & Training
6250 LBJ Freeway
Dallas, TX 75240

Federal Corrections Institution
U.S. Bureau of Prisons
PO Box 1000, Educ. Dept.
Seagoville, TX 75159

Foley's Department Stores
Federated Department Stores
PO Box 1971
Houston, TX 77002

Geophysical Service Inc.
Texas Instruments Inc.
PO Box 225621 M/S 3910
Dallas, TX 75265

Neiman-Marcus
211 N. Ervay, Suite 201
Dallas, TX 75201

Sanger Harris
Federated Dept. Stores
Video/Publications
303 N. Akard
Dallas, TX 75201

Tracor, Inc./Aerospace Austin
Data Management and Training
6500 Tracor Lane, Bldg. 28-13
Austin, TX 78725

U.S. Air Force
A/V Squad.
Det. 1, 1365
Carswell AFB, TX 76127

UTAH

Sunset Sports Centers (UDISCO)
Malone & Hyde, Inc.
2700 S. 900 W.
Salt Lake City, UT 84125

Unisys Corp.
640 N. Sperry Way, EID09
Salt Lake City, UT 84116

VERMONT

Colt Industries
Field Support Group
Fairbanks Weighing Division
711 E. St. Johnsbury Rd.
St. Johnsbury, VT 05819

Northwestern Medical Center
Inservice Dept.
PO Box 1370, Fairfield St.
St. Albans, VT 05478

VIRGINIA

Circuit City Stores, Inc.
Video Production
2040 Thalbro St.
Richmond, VA 23230

Internal Revenue Service
U.S. Treasury Dept.
Training Division
2221 Jefferson Davis Hwy.
Arlington, VA 22202

MCI Communications Corp.
MCI Video Prod. Unit
8003 W. Park Dr.
McLean, VA 22102

Mobil Oil Corp.
Conference Services, Rm. F1-11
3225 Gallows Rd.
Fairfax, VA 22037

Southern States Coop., Inc.
Corp. Communications
6606 W. Broad St.
Richmond, VA 23230

Thalhimer Brothers, Inc.
Carter, Hawley, Hale, Inc.
601 E. Broad St.
Richmond, VA 23219

WASHINGTON

Boeing Aerospace Co.
Learning Center Operations
PO Box 3999 MS 3C-01
Seattle, WA 98124

Rainer National Bank
Rainier BanCorp
Corporate Communications
600 University
Seattle, WA 98101

Safeco Insurance Co.
Education Dept.
Safeco Plaza
Seattle, WA 98185

United Pacific Insurance Co.
Reliance Insurance Group
Human Resources
33405 8th Ave. S., C-3000
Federal Way, WA 98003

Weyerhaeuser Co.
AV-Services
11th and A Sts.
Tacoma, WA 98477

WEST VIRGINIA

Weirton Steel Corp.
Comm. Dept.
M.A.B.
Weirton, WV 26062

WISCONSIN

The Copps Corp.
Personnel Dept.
2828 Wayne St.
Stevens Point, WI 54481

Harley-Davidson Inc.
3700 W. Juneau Ave.
Milwaukee, WI 53201

Kearney & Trecker Corp.
Cross & Trecker Corp.
11000 Theodore Trecker Way
Milwaukee, WI 53214

Kohler Co.
AV/Photo Services
Kohler, WI 53044

Milwaukee Electronic Tool Corp.
Amstar Corp.
13135 W. Lisbon Rd.
Brookfield, WI 53005

Trane Co.
American Standard, Inc.
A/V Svces.
3600 Pammel Creek Rd.
LaCrosse, WI 54601

Wausau Insurance Cos.
PO Box 150
Wausau, WI 54401

APPENDIX B: SALARY SURVEYS

The following organizations publish annual salary survey lists. Organizations usually make the information available to their members as a part of the annual dues.

ITVA Annual Salary Survey

The ITVA annual salary survey is probably the most comprehensive list compiled for the corporate television and freelance side of nonbroadcast television. The survey breaks down compensation by region, job classification, organizational classification, years of experience within major departments, operating budgets, capital budgets, independent (freelance) commission and overall profile of the organization. (ITVA, 6311 N. O'Connor Rd., LB-51, Irving, TX 75039.)

IABC Annual Salary Survey

The IABC annual salary survey breaks down compensation for most audiovisual and business communicator positions. (IABC, One Hallidie Plaza, Suite 600, San Francisco, CA 94102.)

Training Magazine Salary Survey

This survey, published annually by *Training Magazine*, deals mostly with trainers and training-related positions. (Lakewood Publications, 50 S. Ninth Street, Minneapolis, MN 55402.)

APPENDIX C: PROFESSIONAL ORGANIZATIONS

The following professional organizations can be used as great sources for gathering contacts and networking. Most of the listed organizations have local chapters that have regularly scheduled meetings. It is important that you find out which of these organizations have the most to offer you. Then, plan on joining and participating in order to meet people. It is the best way to open doors for your job search.

These organizations also provide services such as newsletters, membership lists, and regional and national conferences—all services that will help you enlarge your contact list. For more information write or call the national office. At the least, the organization will send you membership information; then, you can plan your course of action.

Be aware of local and regional trade groups that are allied with nonbroadcast television. Examples include the Detroit Producers Association, technical writers associations and broadcast groups, such as your local ad club or press club. Information from these organizations is free for the asking.

INTERNATIONAL TELEVISION ASSOCIATION (ITVA)
International Offices
6311 N. O'Connor Rd., LB-51
Irving, TX 75039
(214) 869-1112

The ITVA is the premier professional organization of non-broadcast television people, with over 10,000 members worldwide and growing at the rate of 200 members a month. There are over 90 U.S. chapters that meet monthly; probably one or more are located near you. There are also several student chapters that specialize in helping neophytes in this field.

The ITVA has a job hotline for members only. Other activities include a national convention, monthly newsletters, a membership directory, and local and regional meetings and workshops.

INTERNATIONAL ASSOCIATION OF
BUSINESS COMMUNICATORS (IABC)
Headquarters Office
One Hallidie Plaza
Suite 600
San Francisco, CA 94102
(415) 433-3400

The IABC is an excellent worldwide organization dedicated to business communications and public relations. Its members include communications department managers, public relations directors, writers, (print) editors and audiovisual specialists. It is predominantly a print-oriented organization, but, of late, is broadening its base to include AV and nonbroadcast video. It has over 11,000 members worldwide with 122 local chapters. The IABC operates a Jobline, a telephone hotline that provides up-to-date information on job openings in the field. The IABC also holds a national convention and national, regional and local production competitions. The organization produces monthly newsletters and magazines, distributes an exhaustive membership directory, and has local meetings and workshops to help develop and broaden its membership. There is an affiliated organization for New York members known as the NY/IABC. It publishes a job newsletter for its 650 members.

PUBLIC RELATIONS SOCIETY OF AMERICA (PRSA)
33 Irving Place
New York, NY 10003
(212) 995-2230

The PRSA is a professional society of public relations practitioners with over 13,000 members and more than 90 separate local groups. As a significant number of nonbroadcast television departments are a part of public relations divisions, the importance of this organization to any concerted job search is obvious. PRSA holds a national convention, and many chapters have regular meetings and workshops. Members receive monthly journals and a complete Public Relations Register filled with potential contacts.

ASSOCIATION OF VISUAL COMMUNICATORS (AVC)
900 Palm Ave., Suite B
South Pasadena, CA 91030
(818) 441-2274

The AVC is primarily an association of video production, audio production, multimedia and related industry personnel. Its members include freelancers. Membership is based primarily on both coasts. It is a smaller organization with 600 members.

AUDIO-VISUAL MANAGEMENT ASSOCIATION (AVMA)
7907 N. W. 53 St., Suite 346
Miami, FL 33166
(305) 887-0446

This professional group of business and industrial audiovisual department managers holds semiannual conferences. It is an organization geared to those who already are AV managers and is an excellent source of quality contacts for those in the higher reaches of corporate nonbroadcast television.

ASSOCIATION FOR MULTI-IMAGE (AMI)
8019 N. Himes St., Suite 401
Tampa, FL 33614
(813) 932-1692

The AMI is predominantly a professional organization of 3000 multi-image slide producers and production houses. It has a number of local chapters that offer a good place to expand your contacts. This organization is starting to move into video.

AMERICAN SOCIETY FOR TRAINING AND DEVELOPMENT (ASTD)
Box 1443
1630 Duke St.
Alexandria, VA 22313
(703) 683-8100

The ASTD, with 23,000 members, is the leading professional organization for people involved in the training and development of personnel for industry, government and educational organizations. Its emphasis on instructional technology makes it an organization that should be explored by those who have an interest in the use of nonbroadcast video as a training tool. It holds an annual convention and publishes literature on many media-related topics, such as adult learning theory.

HEALTH SCIENCE COMMUNICATIONS ASSOCIATION (HESCA)
6105 S. Lindell Blvd.
St. Louis, MO 63112
(314) 725-4722

The 800 members of HESCA include hospital and medical college media managers, medical graphic artists, biomedical librarians and health-oriented media producers. It holds an annual national convention with a tape festival and media exhibits. This organization is a good source for those interested in the medical/health area of nonbroadcast video.

NATIONAL ASSOCIATION OF TV ARTS
AND SCIENCES (NATAS)
110 W. 57 St.
New York, NY 10019
(212) 586-8424

The association is made up primarily of people who work in broadcast television. Most cities have active local chapters where you can meet people who can help you move either out of or into nonbroadcast television.

SOCIETY FOR TECHNICAL COMMUNICATIONS (STC)
815 15 St. NW
Washington, DC 20005
(202) 737-0035

With over 12,000 members and more than 100 local chapters, this organization includes all professionals, primarily technical writers, who use technical communications as their primary medium. The organization holds an annual convention and publishes monthly newsletters as well as quarterly journals for those interested in writing.

NATIONAL CABLE TELEVISION ASSOCIATION (NCTA)
1724 Massachusetts Ave. NW
Washington, DC 20036
(202) 775-3550

The NCTA is a professional organization of over 3000 members. Members include franchised CATV operators, programmers, cable networks and related hardware and legal affiliates. In addition to its annual convention, the organization provides reports and newsletters. It publishes "Careers in Cable," a report you should get if you are interested in getting into or moving up within the CATV industry. The booklet entitled "Cable Primer" is a good way to learn about the industry.

NATIONAL ASSOCIATION OF BROADCASTERS (NAB)
1771 N St. NW
Washington, DC 20036
(202) 429-5300

The NAB, with over 7000 members, is the main professional organization for broadcast radio and television stations. Its national convention is the premier showcase for new and prototype video equipment and literally draws tens of thousands of delegates from around the world. It is a great place for contacts, but to get in, you will need credentials as a member or from a vendor or affiliate. The NAB is the lobbying voice for broadcast in America.

INTERNATIONAL COMMUNICATIONS INDUSTRIES ASSOCIATION (ICIA)
3150 Spring St.
Fairfax, VA 22031
(703) 273-7200

The ICIA is an organization of 1500 members drawn primarily from the equipment vendors who service the AV and nonbroadcast markets. It holds a national convention that can be a source for those interested in the hardware side of the industry.

FREELANCE SYNDICATE, INC. (FSI)
P.O. Box 1626
Orem, UT 84057
(801) 785-1300

This is a relatively new organization of more than 2000 free-lance writers, graphic artists and photographers. The FSI seeks to enhance the viability of freelance as a career. It operates a computer network to exchange information and completed work among members.

Bibliography

BOOKS

Bolles, Richard. *What Color Is Your Parachute?* Berkeley, CA: Ten Speed Press, 1982?

Bone, Jan. *Opportunities in Cable TV.* Lincolnwood, IL: National Textbook Co., 1984.

Broadcasting/Cablecasting Yearbook. Washington, DC: Broadcasting Publications, Inc., annual.

Brush, Judith M. and Douglas P. *Private Television Communications: The New Directions.* Cold Springs, NY: HI Press, Inc., 1986.

Cable Contracts Yearbook. NY: Larimi Communications Associates, Ltd., annual.

Denny, Jon S. *Careers in Cable TV.* NY: Harper & Row, Inc., 1983.

Half, Robert. *The Robert Half Way to Get Hired in Today's Job Market.* NY: Rawson, Wade, 1981.

Jackson, Tom. *The Perfect Resume.* NY: Doubleday, 1981.

Levering, Robert. *A Great Place to Work: What Makes Some Employers So Good and Most So Bad.* NY: Random House, 1988.

Malloy, John. *Dress for Success.* NY: Warner Books, 1976.

Morris, William, and Caberra, James. *How to Survive the Loss of a Job and Find Another Successfully.* Orlando, FL: Harcourt Brace Jovanovich, 1987.

Noronha, Shonan F. R. *Careers in Communications.* Lincolnwood, IL: National Textbook Co., 1987.

Reed, Jean. *Resumes That Get Jobs*, 4th ed. NY: Arco Publishing Co., 1986.

261

Sapan, Joshua. *Making it in Cable TV.* NY: Perigree Books, 1984.
Smith, Michael H. *The Resume Writers Handbook.* NY: Harper & Row, 1987.
The Standard Directory of Advertising Agencies (The Red Book). Wilmette, IL: National Register Publishing Co., published every February, June and October.
Stokes, Judith Tereno. *The Business of Nonbroadcast Television.* White Plains, NY: Knowledge Industry Publications, Inc., 1988.
Video Register and Teleconferencing Resources Directory. White Plains, NY: Knowledge Industry Publications, Inc., 1989.

PERIODICALS

Feedback (Health Sciences Communications Association, 6105 Lindell Blvd., St. Louis, MO 63112).
Journal of Biomedical Communications (Health Sciences Communications Association, 6105 Lindell Blvd., St. Louis, MO 63112).
Telespan Newsletter (50 W. Palm St., Altadena, CA 91001).

Index

Advertising, 48, 224-226
Advanced career options, 7-8
Asking questions, 123-130
Assessing your career, 156-158
Association of Biomedical
    Communications Directors
    (ABCD), 46
Association of Multi-Image
    (AMI), 97
Audiovisual specialist, 193-
    194

Body language, 103-104
Broadcast television, 228-231
Brush Report, The, 42, 59

Consumer services, 53-55
Contact sheets, 165-167
Corporate (industrial)
    television, 41-45
  careers in, 42-45
Corporation for Public
    Broadcasting (CPB), 32
Counteroffers, 158-160

Director, 200-202

Editor, 188-190
Educational television, 30–40
  applications, 33–35
  careers in, 35–39
  contacts, 39–40
  distribution, 30–32
  employment prospects, 40
  on campus, 77–78
  scope of, 32–33
Entry-level positions, 7
Engineer, 196-199

Feature-Accomplishment-
    Benefit (FAB) approach,
    86-89
Freelancers, 51-53, 73-74,
    215-217
  contacts, 53
  decision, 219
  future prospects, 53, 217
  pros and cons, 218

Graphic designer, 194-195

Handling objections, 173-178

Health and medical
    institutions, 45
  careers in, 46-47
  prospects, 48
Health Sciences Communica-
    tions Association (HESCA),
    46

Interactive video, 17-19
International Association of
    Business Communication
    (IABC), 48, 97
International Television
    Association (ITVA), 1, 97
Internships, 79-81
Interview attire, 101-103
Interview questions, 112-117

Looking-for-a-job axioms,
    160-173

Makeup artist, 209-210
Manager or media department
    director, 206-208
Management Recruiters
    International, 3, 75
Motivation questions, 119-121

Narrowcasting, 15-16
National Center for Education
    Statistics (NCES), 32
Networking, 86, 221
Nonbroadcast television
  applications, 4-7
  audience acceptance of, 14-
    15

Nonbroadcast television (cont.)
  definition of, 4
  evolution of, 9-13
  industry acceptance of, 13-14
  users, 15-19
Nonbroadcast video
    professionals case studies,
    19-27

Personality questions, 117-119
Producer, 202-204
Production houses, 49
  careers in, 49-50
  contacts in, 50
  employment prospects 50-51
Production or technical
    assistant, 182-185
Professional organizations, 97
Public relations, 48, 226-228
Public Relations Society of
    America (PRSA), 48, 97

Qualifications briefs, 143-148
  employment history, 145
  educational background,
    146-147
  miscellaneous, 147-148
  preparation, 142

Radio and audio studios, 231-
    232
Reliance Electric, 2
Resumes
  dos and don'ts, 140-143
  features, 133-140
  unsolicited, 131-133

Resume reels, 148-153

Salary, 121-123
Supervisor, 204-206

Talents, 210
Technician, 195-196
Teleconferencing, 16-17

Temporary employment, 74-75

Videographer, 184-188
Volunteer experience, 75-77

Writer, 190-193

ABOUT THE AUTHOR

Ken Jurek is currently the director of video and communications for Management Recruiters International, Inc. He began his professional life selling radio advertising time and eventually joined Cuyahoga Community College as a production assistant. He eventually became department head and tenured professor in audiovisual technology and library media technology as well as manager of the instructional television unit for the campus. Eight years ago, he moved to industry and started the video department at MRI.

Ken Jurek also writes "On a Personal Note" column for *Video Manager* and has articles appearing in other magazines. His knowledge of hiring and productivity comes from the past 10 years of study and 20 years of practical on-line supervision and leadership.

He lives on a farm in Richfield, OH, with his wife, Joan, who is an editor-director. In addition to raising Nubian goats and domestic geese, Ken is a beekeeper. Regarding the tending of bees, he says philosophically, "After you've dealt with 100,000 angry honey bees, people are no problem!"